DATE DUE

GAYLORD			PRINTED IN U.S.A.

DIE MEISTERSINGER
VON NÜRNBERG

VON

RICHARD WAGNER

———

WITH

INTRODUCTION, NOTES, AND VOCABULARY

BY

W. P. BIGELOW,

ASSOCIATE PROFESSOR OF GERMAN AND MUSIC
AMHERST COLLEGE

———

AMERICAN BOOK COMPANY
NEW YORK-:-CINCINNATI-:-CHICAGO

PREFACE

GOETHE once said to a friend, "Wäre ich jung und ver-. wegen genug, so würde ich absichtlich gegen alle tech- nischen Grillen verstossen, ich würde Alliterationen, Asso- nanzen, und falsche Reime, alles gebrauchen, wie es mir käme und bequem wäre, aber ich würde auf die Hauptsache losgehen, und so gute Dinge zu sagen suchen, dass jeder geneigt sein sollte, es zu lesen, und auswendig lernen."

Richard Wagner was "young and audacious" enough to do just this. He created his own precedents, he made his own rules, he developed his own theories simultaneously with his own work. In fact, contrary to the usual method of procedure, his theories were the result of his work. *Parsifal*, the high- est development of his methods, is far removed from *Tann- häuser*, though the germs of the former are clearly evident in the latter. He demanded a drama which should be mu- sical and a music which should be dramatic. He dreamed of a perfect, supreme art-work, which should gather to itself and combine all the other arts and accessories, music, speech, word-painting, acting, scenery, time, circumstance, and place, all of which should contribute to the one grand end, lofty dramatic expression. Consequently, if one wishes to form a correct judgment of Wagner's achievements, he must study each work as a united, inseparable whole. Schelling says : "In a true art-work, there is no such thing as a single beauty. Only the whole is beautiful, and he, who cannot raise himself to the point of contemplating the work as a whole, is totally unfit to pass judgment."

3

Wagner's dramas were never written merely to be read, for they are idealized speech, speech idealized and made radiant by music, and without the music they might be compared to unilluminated transparencies. The words were made for the music, no less than the music for the words, and that is the reason why much in the text is so unusual, peculiar, and untranslatable. It is a unique species, this art-work of Wagner's, and demands a peculiar language. Who are the inhabitants of the world into which he transports us? They are gods, goddesses, demi-gods, giants, dwarfs, heroes, supernatural beings, both above and below us moderns, outside of our laws, our conventions and limitations. They belong to the realm of myth, fancy, and imagination, and why should they not speak a strange and new language? How could the great singing creatures of the *Nibelungen Trilogy* use our modern pigmy speech? It would sound ridiculous if they did. Like Lessing, Goethe and Schiller, Wagner created a language for his own purpose. He was able to live himself back into the times and atmosphere of his characters. He spoke their language, and for this language he found music to interpret it to our modern times. As Nietzsche says, "He forced language back to its original state, when it expressed itself not in ideas, but in poetry, picture and feeling."

The music drama to which this volume is devoted differs from all the other Wagner dramas in that the characters appearing in it are not mythical personages or emanations of the poet's brain, but are real flesh and blood. Of all operas, *Die Meistersinger von Nürnberg* is the one German opera. It is to the realm of opera what Bach's *Matthaeus Passion*, Beethoven's *Missa Solemnis*, or the Cologne Cathedral are in their respective spheres, a representative work, a product distinctively German. No other drama has ever revealed to us such an accurate, genuine, sympathetic picture of German life. Never has any artist been able to paint in such attractive colors, or to surround with such genial humor and poetic beauty a comparatively unattractive and prosaic period of national life. The German race above all others seems to present a striking mixture of idealism and materialism, and nowhere is this contrast more clearly defined, and the struggle between these two seemingly antagonistic traits so vividly delineated, as in this very work. Wagner effects a reconciliation of these contrasted and hostile elements by a harmonious development of life through art.

Therefore, notwithstanding the incompleteness which must necessarily attend the study of these dramas through the text alone, the editor believes that there is time and place in the American college curriculum for the study of such forceful and epoch making works. At least the opportunity and incentive should not be lacking, and this, supplemented by frequent hearing of the entire work in later life, will furnish an element of culture and enlightenment, which is conspicuously wanting in America when compared with other lands.

In the preparation of this volume, the editor claims nothing more than to have collected and carefully sifted the large body of literature on the subject and, as far as possible in such a limited space, to have incorporated what seemed best adapted to his purpose. Among the authorities consulted are Ambros, Langhans, Neumann, Chamberlain, von Hagen, von Wolzogen, Mey, Phol, and many others, to whom the editor acknowledges his indebtedness.

It is further my pleasure to thank Prof. J. F. Genung of Amherst College for his generous assistance in the preparation of this volume. He has read the entire proof and his suggestions have been many and valuable.

Amherst College.   W. P. B.

... bin in Ruh'
Hans Sachs ein Schuh-
macher und Poet dazu.

INTRODUCTION

IN order to understand and appreciate any great work of art, it is necessary to put one's self back into the times and conditions in which the author found his material and inspiration. Especially is this true of such a work as *Die Meistersinger von Nürnberg* by Richard Wagner, the poet-musician, in which he sought to deal with the present by a caricature of the past. Such an historical retrospect as this takes us back to the time when there were no printing presses, hence no notes, singing books, or sheet music, no pianos, no manual of harmony, no "artists," as we understand the word, hence no concerts or recitals; nothing like rhythm or beat, in the modern sense, for there were no notes to express them. Everything was without form, primitive and emotional. "Spring's command and sweet necessity moved him, he sang because he must."

Under the lovely skies of southern France, in the garden-like land where vineyards, olive and almond trees cover the earth in luxuriant abundance, where womanly beauty and knightly chivalry lend a glamour to existence, there grew up in the eleventh century a school of singers known to us of modern times as the "Troubadours," called thus because they composed or found (*trouver*) their own songs. These noble personages, however, did not deign to sing their compositions, but intrusted this function to trained attendants, called "Jongleurs" or "Minstrels." Their songs portrayed, for the most part, deeds of chivalry and passion, and were full of exuberant, extravagant gallantry.

This same spirit manifested itself in Germany in the type of the "Minnesinger." But he, unlike his counterpart of the "Troubadour," sang as well as composed his own songs. His themes were the spring, the flowers, the songs of birds, and idealized womanhood.

The intellectual life of any nation may be compared to

the endless succession of seasons; a sunny period of growth and harvest is followed by decay and icy winter, during which the mental life of an entire nation may seem to slumber and die. The last part of the thirteenth century saw the blossoming time of the Troubadours and Minnesingers give way to the icy winter of the dark Middle Ages. In Germany the political conditions were especially unfavorable. The ruling house of the Habsburgs had very little sympathy with the intellectual life of its subjects, and the nobles and knights had sunk to the level of common highwaymen, and poetry and music no longer found a hospitable home in their castles. But toward the end of the fifteenth century, two events occurred which were to dispel the terrible darkness in which Germany had been wrapped for over a hundred years. First, the invention of printing; second, the capture of Constantinople by the Turks and the consequent expulsion of the Greek scholars there, who, wandering into western lands, kindled again the torch of classical research, which was to light the way to a more humane age, and eventually to bring about the Reformation. The Americas were discovered, commerce was exalted, and thus gradually the whole situation was changed. Courts and castles ceased to be, as of yore, the promoters of art. The monasteries were no longer the centers of learning, and research, but yielded these functions to flourishing cities and towns. This revival of intellectual activity, however, did not restore the old romantic and sentimental conception of life, which the poetry of chivalry and the atmosphere of the courts had generated, but in its place there arose a cool, prosaic, matter-of-fact mode of thought which left but little room for poetic expression. It was during this period that the art of the Mastersingers arose and developed, and from this period Wagner drew his material. Popular poetry disappeared only to reappear in the form of the German folk-song. Artistic poetry left the castles of knights and nobles for the lowly abode of the citizens of the town. And these Mastersingers, these honest craftsmen, did the best they could, but they were, of course, at best, able only to imitate the external form of their models. They did not have the light, graceful style of romantic poetry. Their poetry, like themselves, was coarse, stiff, and pedantic. It had, however, its genial side.

After a hard day's work, tired and oppressed by care and anxiety, they would gather together, and in the practice of their "blissful art" forget their worry and trouble. To Walter's question:

> "If then so much your rules are prized,
> By what man were they first devised?"

Wagner makes Sachs reply thus:

> "By certain sorely troubled masters,
> Their hearts oppressed by life's disasters,
> By suffering overweighted,
> That they might take it, and ever make it
> A memory of youthful love
> In which the soul of spring shall move."

They founded schools and guilds, and verse-craft became one of the incorporated trades in nearly all the German cities. These schools or guilds sought to raise the mental and moral standards of the youth through the discipline which their rules enforced. But in the course of time, by placing an undue stress on forms at the expense of matter, and by hedging themselves about with hard and fast rules, they became little better than conceited pedants, without life or possibility of progress; and it is this feature that Wagner has sought to satirize in his opera.

The first Mastersingers are said to have been the following twelve men, all of whom lived in the tenth century, during the reign of Emperor Otto I:

Heinrich Frauenlob,	Doctor of Divinity.
Heinrich Mögling,	" "
Nicolaus Klingsohr,	" "
The strong Poppo or Poppser,	Glassblower.
Walther von der Vogelweide,	Land owner.
Wolfgang Rohn or Rahn,	Knight.
Hanns Ludwig Marner,	Nobleman.
Barthel Regenbogen,	Blacksmith.
Sigmar der Weise,	von Zwickau.
Conrad Geiger,	Musician.
N. Cantzler,	Tablemaker.
Stefan Stoll,	Ropemaker.

This interesting list of "poets" needs no comment.

These men by their enthusiastic efforts spread the practice of the "blissful art" through all the cities of middle and south Germany; and before long Nürnberg, Mainz, Strassburg, and other cities in that region enjoyed the reputation of being centers of the Mastersingers' art. It can easily be seen how, with the ever increasing membership of the guilds, a more careful organization became necessary. Accordingly, about the end of the fifteenth century a code was issued which contained rules and prohibitions pertaining to the regulation of their efforts and proceedings. This was the *Tabulatur*. There was also another book which passed upon their business transactions.

Proficiency in the knowledge demanded by the *Tabulatur* decided the rank of the members of the Guild. One who had partially mastered it was "Schüler" (*scholar*). One who had completely mastered it was "Schulfreund" (*schoolman*). One who knew some of the "tones" was "Singer." One who composed a poem to a "tone" already existing was "Dichter" (*poet*), and one who composed both words and melody was a "Meistersinger" or *Master*.

The twelve men whom Wagner uses as characters were noted Mastersingers who lived in Nürnberg about the middle of the seventeenth century. Their meetings were held on Sundays and holidays in St. Catherine's Church immediately after the afternoon service. These meetings were of two kinds, the "Freisingen," which was non-competitive, and the "Hauptsingen," which was competitive, during which latter a "Merker" (*marker*), ensconced behind a curtain, noted down on a slate the candidate's mistakes. Seven mistakes were allowed, but one who made more was declared "versungen und vertan" (*outsung and outdone*). Whoever wished to be admitted to the guild must find a master to vouch for his respectability, and then sing before all the members. If the candidate passed, he was decorated with a silver chain and badge, the latter representing King David playing upon his harp, and was then admitted to the guild. Furthermore, candidates were apprenticed to members of the guild and were instructed by them free of charge in the different modes and tones. David was thus apprenticed to Sachs.

"Tones" (*Töne*) denoted the scheme of versification, *i.e.*

meter, accent, feet, etc. "Modes" (*Weisen*) were melodies to which the verses were sung. There were hundreds of these tones and modes, and each one had its own peculiar name. A master must know them all by heart and be able to sing them.

A complete "Mastersong" usually consisted of three "Bars" or staves. A "Bar" was made up of three "Gesätze," or stanzas, which in turn were made up of two "Stollen," or shorter stanzas in like meter and melody. The first Gesatz was immediately followed by an "Abgesang" (*aftersong*), which must be different in meter and length from the preceding stanza, and sung to a different melody. Walther's song constructed under Hans Sachs' direction will serve for illustration; see pages 103-4-5-6, 115-16. Pages 103 and 104 contain the first "Gesätz" and its "Abgesang." Page 105 contains the second "Gesätz" and its "Abgesang." Pages 115 and 116 the third "Gesätz" and its "Abgesang."

Rhymeless lines, *i. e.* lines standing alone, were called "Waisen." Lines rhyming with a line in the following stanza were called "Körner."

Monosyllabic words, standing alone but constituting an entire line and rhyming with another line of the same sort and similarly situated, were called "Pausen." Dissyllabic words under the same circumstances were called "Schlagreime."

In general, monosyllabic rhymes were called "Stumpfe," and dissyllabic were called "Klingende."

The model and standard of expression was Martin Luther's *Bible*.

Some thirty-two faults were specified in the *Tabulatur;* the most flagrant as follows :

"Milben;" mistakes brought about by the abbreviation or ellipsis of a word for the sake of rhyme, *e. g.*

> "Von diesem Dinge
> Will ich jetzo singe(n)."

"Lind und Hart;" a mistake in rhyming a hard and a soft word, *e. g.* "Knaben" and "Knappen," "Tod" and "Gott."

"Klebsilben;" a contraction of two syllables into one, *e. g.* "Kein" for "Keinen," "zur" for "zu der," etc.

"Blinde Meinung" (*Cloudy Meaning*); sometimes by omitted conjunction.

"Blind Wort;" unintelligible words as "Sag" for "Sach," "sig" for "sich," etc.

"Aequivoca;" words of double meaning or words spelled alike, but of different meaning.

"Laster;" faulty rhyme.

"Unredbare Wörter;" unsingable phrases.

"Falsch Gebänd;" faulty versification.

A singer must choose a key within the register of his voice. A single line must not contain more than thirteen syllables, because more than that could not be sung in a single breath. These few instances will serve to show the extremely mechanical nature of their artistic requirements.

Just how Wagner came to choose this seemingly unpromising material for a comic opera, he himself tells us in a pamphlet published in 1851, entitled *Eine Mitteilung an meine Freunde*. Wagner writes : "Immediately after finishing *Tannhäuser* (1845), I found myself at liberty to visit a Bohemian bathing resort for the benefit of my health. Here, as upon all occasions when I have been able to withdraw myself from the air of the footlights and from my duties in such an atmosphere, I soon began to be possessed by a light and joyous mood. For the first time a gaiety, peculiar to my character and with artistic significance, began to stir within me. Almost involuntarily, I had a short time before resolved that my next work should be a comic opera. Now I think of it, this determination may have resulted in part from the advice of well-meaning friends who counseled me to write an opera of a more "popular" character, because they agreed that this would procure my recognition on the German stage and secure that success, for the continued lack of which my financial condition was becoming very distressing." Then he goes on to tell how upon the journey there came to him the picture of a comic play, which might serve as a sort of satirical supplement to his singing contest at the Wartburg (*Tannhäuser*). This picture was *Die Meistersinger von Nürnberg*, with Hans Sachs at their head. In regard to Hans Sachs he says further : "I conceived Hans Sachs as the last appearance of the art-producing folk-spirit, and in that character I contrasted him with the extremely droll and tabulatur-poetical pedantry of which I gave a personal expression in the character of the 'Marker.'"

From this letter the entire plan of the drama may be seen, just as it unfolded itself in the mind of the poet. In the foreground the worthy masters, among them in sharp contrast, Beckmesser, the master and pedant, Pogner, the rich blacksmith, and Sachs, the cobbler-poet. All the less pleasant and at the same time comical features of the Mastersingers are embodied in the person of the "Marker." The narrow-minded illiberality, the matter-of-fact conception of poetry, attaching itself only to the forms, are here united with unmeasured vanity and petty jealousy, thus forming a character which, thanks to the exquisite humor that pervades it, has not only a repulsive, but an infinitely comical effect. Veit Pogner is the contrast. In him the good features of the Mastersingers find their embodiment. He is not a poet, it is true, but he is a typical citizen of the wealthy art-loving Nürnberg, who, compelled by a warm love of art, offers the hand of his only daughter, together with his worldly goods, to the Master who shall be victorious in the contest of St. John's day. Lastly, Hans Sachs. He is "the only truly original and productive figure" in the circle of the "Mastersingers." As a poet he stands in complete opposition to the dull craftsman-like conception of poetry, to which all the other Mastersingers adhere. As a man, too, he is such a splendid, genial, thoroughly sympathetic figure, mild and kind, self-denying, as evinced by his kindness to the lovers, although he dearly loves Eva himself: a warm patriot, an enthusiastic champion of intellectual progress. Of all the characters we meet with in the works of Wagner, Hans Sachs is the one who stands nearest to our hearts. And then the love of Eva and Walther, the trial and failure before the Masters, the evening serenade, the final triumph of youth and individual genius :—these were the elements of the drama, which out of the obscure, unpromising historical background of the old Mastersinger guilds, arose before the vision of the poet and were welded into this unique art-work.

But the task was not to be finished at once. Wagner's impetuous, inexhaustible genius allowed him no rest. *Tristan*

und Isolde, Der Ring des Nibelungen, were already burning in
his soul, colossal undertakings either of them alone. The
pain of exile, his terrible mental isolation, his sufferings even
of hunger, were conditions which were not conducive to
mental activity along humorous lines, and it was not until
twenty years later that the musical portion of the work was
taken up with anything like his characteristic energy. Baited
by foes, outlawed by society, exposed defenceless to the bit-
terest attacks of narrow-minded critics, this much-tried
genius could but stand helplessly by and hear his much
cherished art principles derided by those in power in the
theatrical world. The press almost without exception was
inimical. *"Wenn Musik stinken könnte, so würde man bei dieser Ecorcherie in Noten die Nase zuhalten müssen,"* is a fair
specimen of the press notices concerning the night brawl at
the end of the second act. The word *"Meistersinger"* was
wittily written "Meisterschinder;" in fact, books of consider-
able size have been published in later days, containing alpha-
betical lists of the epithets applied to Wagner by the critics
of his time.

It was the royal art-loving Ludwig of Bavaria who finally
freed this genius from his martyrdom and brought light and
warmth into his life. In 1868, under the patronage of this
monarch, Wagner had the satisfaction of seeing the *Mastersingers* adequately rendered in the royal theater at Munich
under the direction of Hans von Bülow. From that time on
the world began to hear, feel, and comprehend, and to-day
the whole civilized world unites in rendering the homage due
to this unique genius.

There can be no doubt that the contrast between the
narrow-minded art-pedantry of the other Mastersingers and
the spontaneous art as embodied in Hans Sachs and Walther
form a parallel to the combat which Wagner had to fight
with the no less narrow-minded critics of his own time. To
quote from his own writings again: "Out of the ironical
consciousness of the artist who with his ideal has to face a
public which misunderstands him, and an inimical host of
critics, there arose during my stay in Bohemia the sketch of
the *Mastersingers.*"* Even to-day, especially here in America, we hear the same old criticism:

* Richard Wagner's *Lebensbericht,* page 35.

> "Not one full close, no grace notes you see,
> And not a trace of melody."

Through Sachs he says:

> "One way you measure solely,
> A work your rules do not fit;
> Resign your own views wholly,
> Some other rules apply to it."

And he utters his own creed when he says:

> "The melody do you think no matter,
> Both words and notes should fit the song."

It is not at all difficult to see why *Die Meistersinger* is pre-eminently a folk-opera, when we consider that up to Wagner's time grand opera had had to do chiefly with kings, courts, courtiers, parasites, and puppets; that in them a sphere of life had been pictured of which the ordinary man knew nothing except as he read about it or had been told it in the form of a fairy tale, certainly a life in which he had never participated. When we consider the trifling and inconsequent nature of the librettos, wherein a lace handkerchief, a silver slipper, or the intrigues of a courtesan constituted the principal matter for contemplation, all this combined with a music absolutely purposeless except as it was written to please some vain singer or flatter some monarch, and then, too, the pointless ballet, the strutting gallant, the heavy villain, the deceitful housemaid, all strung together like keys on a ring,—it is easy to see how far ordinary grand opera was removed from the life of the people. But in the *Mastersingers* the people found themselves again. The artisans, the laborers, are real flesh and blood. Yes, the very labor itself, by which they were wont to earn their daily bread, is there too. They behold their own philosophy unfolded, their poetry revealed, even to themselves. Hans Sachs is their representative, and Walther, their chosen leader, is made one of them on the common ground of art. When in the last act Walther sings the prize song with such fervor and beauty that it warms their very hearts, Wagner, with magnificent use of the means at his command, makes it seem as though the whole assembly, fired with the poet's inspiration, became poets themselves; and one by one, almost unconsciously, they begin to sing softly with Walther, and masters, apprentices, common people, everybody, all sing and swell the volume of sound into a chorus of overwhelming grandeur and beauty, all united and for the moment equal on the common ground of art.

It is no longer merely a prize-song sung by an individual, but rather the universal, spontaneous homage to the art which all alike love. And when Walther, true to his traditions, refuses the master's badge, the wise and sympathetic Hans Sachs in a few words knows how to complete the reconciliation between the knight and the peasants. And there he stands, as the curtain falls, Hans Sachs, the incarnate reconciliation of Idealism and Materialism through art.

PERSONEN DER HANDLUNG

Hans Sachs, Schuster,
Veit Pogner, Goldschmied,
Kunz Vogelgesang, Kürschner,
Konrad Nachtigal, Spengler,
Sixtus Beckmesser, Schreiber,
Fritz Kothner, Bäcker, } Meister-
Balthasar Zorn, Zinngiesser, singer.
Ulrich Eisslinger, Würzkrämer,
Augustin Moser, Schneider,
Hermann Ortel, Seifensieder,
Hans Schwarz, Strumpfwirker,
Hans Foltz, Kupferschmied,
Walther von Stolzing, ein junger Ritter aus Franken.
David, Sachsens Lehrbube.
Eva, Pogners Tochter.
Magdalene, Evas Amme.
Ein Nachtwächter.

Bürger und Frauen aller Zünfte. Gesellen. Lehrbuben.
Mädchen. Volk.

Nürnberg.
Um die Mitte des 16. Jahrhunderts.

ERSTER AUFZUG

The stage presents an oblique section of the interior of St. Catherine's Church. The nave of the church is supposed to extend back toward the left, and only the last rows of seats are visible. The foreground of the stage encloses the open space before the choir, which is later on shut off from the nave by a curtain.

As the curtain rises, the congregation is singing with organ accompaniment the last verse of a "Chorale," which closes the afternoon service introductory to the Feast of St. John.

Choral der Gemeinde

Da zu dir der Heiland kam,
willig deine Taufe nahm,
weihte sich dem Opfertod,
gab er uns des Heil's Gebot :
5   dass wir durch dein' Tauf' uns weih'n,
seines Opfers wert zu sein.
    Edler Täufer,
    Christ's Vorläufer !
Nimm uns freundlich an,
10   dort am Fluss Jordan.

During the "Chorale" and its interludes the following pantomimic scene, accompanied by orchestra:

In the last rows of seats are seated *Eva* and *Magdalene*. *Walther von Stolzing* stands at some distance leaning against a pillar, gazing intently at *Eva*. She repeatedly turns round toward the knight and answers his now imploring, now tender looks of love and entreaty timidly and modestly, but tenderly and encouragingly. *Magdalene* pauses frequently in her worship to nudge *Eva* reprovingly and to caution her. As the Chorale comes to an end, and during a somewhat long postlude by the organ, the congregation gradually leaves the church by the main door, which is supposed to be at the left toward the background. *Walther* steps quickly up to the two women, who have likewise risen and have turned toward the exit.

Walther (softly but fervently to *Eva*).

Verweilt ! — Ein Wort ! Ein einzig Wort !

1. **dir** = St. John.

19

Eva (turning quickly to *Magdalene*).

Mein Brusttuch! Schau! Wohl liegt's im Ort?

Magdalene

Vergesslich Kind! Nun heisst es: such'!
(She goes back to the seats.)

Walther

Fräulein! Verzeiht der Sitte Bruch!
Eines zu wissen, eines zu fragen,
5 was nicht müsst' ich zu brechen wagen?
Ob Leben oder Tod? Ob Segen oder Fluch?
Mit einem Worte sei mir's vertraut: —
mein Fräulein, sagt —

Magdalene (returning).
Hier ist das Tuch.

Eva

O weh! die Spange!

Magdalene
Fiel sie wohl ab?

(She goes back again, looking along the floor.)

Walther

10 Ob Licht und Lust, oder Nacht und Grab?
Ob ich erfahr', wonach ich verlange,
ob ich vernehme, wovor mir graut: —
Mein Fräulein, sagt —

Magdalene (again returning).
Da ist auch die Spange. —
Komm', Kind! Nun hast du Spang' und Tuch. —
15 O weh! da vergass ich selbst mein Buch!
(She goes back again.)

Walther

Dies eine Wort, ihr sagt mir's nicht?
Die Silbe, die mein Urteil spricht?
Ja, oder: Nein! — ein flücht'ger Laut:
mein Fräulein, sagt, seid ihr schon Braut?

1. **Mein ... Ort:** a mere device to be alone with Walther.   2. **Vergesslich:** such abbreviated forms, of common occurrence in all poetry, are especially frequent in the Wagner texts.   9. **Spange:** another device.

Magdalene
(already having returned, bows to *Walther*).

Sieh da, Herr Ritter?
Wie sind wir hochgeehrt:
mit Evchens Schutze
habt ihr euch gar beschwert?
Darf den Besuch des Helden
ich Meister Pogner melden?

Walther
(passionately).

Betrat ich doch nie sein Haus!

Magdalene

Ei! Junker! Was sagt ihr da aus!
In Nürnberg eben nur angekommen,
war't ihr nicht freundlich aufgenommen?
Was Küch' und Keller, Schrein und Schrank
euch bot, verdient' es keinen Dank?

Eva

Gut Lenchen! Ach! das meint er ja nicht.
Doch von mir wohl wünscht er Bericht —
wie sag' ich's schnell? — Versteh' ich's doch kaum! —
Mir ist, als wär' ich gar im Traum! —
Er fragt, — ob ich schon Braut?

Magdalene (looking round cautiously).

Hilf Gott! Sprich nicht so laut!
Jetzt lass' uns nach Hause gehn;
wenn uns die Leut' hier sehn!

Walther

Nicht eher, bis ich alles weiss!

Eva

's ist leer, die Leut' sind fort.

Magdalene

Drum eben wird mir heiss! —
Herr Ritter, an and'rem Ort!

David enters from the sacristy and occupies himself drawing together dark colored curtains, which shut off obliquely the foreground from the nave.

7. **Betrat ... Haus:** a wish. 13. **gut:** see p. 20, l. 2; **Lenchen** = Magdalene.

Walther

Nein ! Erst dies Wort !

Eva (holding *Magdalene*).

Dies Wort ?

Magdalene (having already turned away, beholds *David*
and speaks his name tenderly aside).

David ? Ei ! David hier ?

Eva (urgently).

Was sag' ich ? Sag' du's mir !

Magdalene (absent-mindedly looking round frequently
at *David*).

Herr Ritter, was ihr die Jungfer fragt,
5 das ist so leichtlich nicht gesagt ;
fürwahr ist Evchen Pogner Braut —

Eva (quickly interrupting).

Doch hat noch keiner den Bräut'gam erschaut.

Magdalene

Den Bräut'gam wohl noch niemand kennt,
bis morgen ihn das Gericht ernennt,
10 das dem Meistersinger erteilt den Preis —

Eva (as before).

Und selbst die Braut ihm reicht das Reis.

Walther

Dem Meistersinger ?

Eva (timidy).

Seid ihr das nicht ?

Walther

Ein Werbgesang ?

Magdalene

Vor Wettgericht.

Walther

Den Preis gewinnt ?

Magdalene

Wen die Meister meinen.

Walther

15 Die Braut dann wählt ?

11. **das Reis**: symbol of victory.

Eva (forgetting herself).

Euch, oder keinen!

(*Walther* turns aside in great excitement, walking up and down.)

Magdalene (very much shocked).

Was? Evchen! Evchen! Bist du von Sinnen?

Eva

Gut' Lene! hilf mir den Ritter gewinnen!

Magdalene

Sah'st ihn doch gestern zum ersten Mal?

Eva

Das eben schuf mir so schnelle Qual,
5 dass ich schon längst ihn im Bilde sah: —
sag', trat er nicht ganz wie David nah'?

Magdalene

Bist du toll? Wie David?

Eva

Wie David im Bild.

Magdalene

Ach! meinst du den König mit der Harfen
und langem Bart in der Meister Schild?

Eva

10 Nein! der, dess' Kiesel den Goliath warfen,
das Schwert im Gurt, die Schleuder zur Hand:
von lichten Locken das Haupt umstrahlt,
wie ihn uns Meister Dürer gemalt.

Magdalene (sighing loudly).

Ach, David! David!

David (who has gone out and just returned again, a rule in his belt, and swinging in his hand a large piece of white chalk on the end of a string).

Da bin ich! Wer ruft?

Magdalene

15 Ach, David! Was ihr für Unglück schuft!
(Aside.)
Der liebe Schelm! wüsst' er's noch nicht?
(Aloud.)
Ei, seht! da hat er uns gar verschlossen?

David (tenderly to *Magdalene*)

Ins Herz euch allein!

Magdalene (aside).

Das treue Gesicht! —
(Aloud.)

Mein sagt! Was treibt ihr hier für Possen?

David

Behüt' es! Possen? Gar ernste Ding'!
Für die Meister hier richt' ich den Ring.

Magdalene

5 Wie? Gäb' es ein Singen?

David

Nur Freiung heut':
der Lehrling wird da losgesprochen,
der nichts wider die Tabulatur verbrochen;
Meister wird, wen die Prob' nicht reu't.

Magdalene

Da wär' der Ritter ja am rechten Ort. —
10 Jetzt, Evchen, komm', wir müssen fort.

Walther (turning quickly to the women).

Zu Meister Pogner lasst mich euch geleiten.

Magdalene

Erwartet den hier; er ist bald da.
Wollt ihr euch Evchens Hand erstreiten,
rückt Ort und Zeit das Glück euch nah'.
(Two *Apprentices* enter bringing benches.)
15   Jetzt eilig von hinnen!

Walther

Was soll ich beginnen?

Magdalene

Lasst David euch lehren,
die Freiung begehren. —
Davidchen! hör', mein lieber Gesell,
20 den Ritter bewahr' hier wohl zur Stell'!
Was Fein's aus der Küch'
bewahr' ich für dich:

---

1. **Ins ... allein:** understand *verschlossen* in the previous line

und morgen begehr' du noch dreister,
wird heut' der Junker hier Meister.
(She hurries toward the door.)

Eva (to *Walther*).

Seh' ich euch wieder?

Walther (ardently).

Heut' abend, gewiss! —
Was ich will wagen,
5   wie könnt' ich's sagen?
Neu ist mein Herz, neu mein Sinn,
neu ist mir alles, was ich beginn'.
Eines nur weiss ich:
eines begreif' ich:
10   mit allen Sinnen
euch zu gewinnen!
Ist's mit dem Schwert nicht, muss es gelingen,
gilt es als Meister euch zu ersingen.
Für euch Gut und Blut!
15   Für euch
Dichters heil'ger Mut!

Eva (with great fervor).

Mein Herz, sel'ger Glut,
    für euch
liebesheil'ge Hut!

Magdalene

20 Schnell heim, sonst geht's nicht gut!

David (looking *Walther* over).

Gleich Meister? Oho! viel Mut!

(*Magdalene* pulls *Eva* away quickly through the curtains.)
Walther, perturbed and brooding, has thrown himself into an elevated ecclesiastical arm-chair, which two *Apprentices* have moved from the wall toward the center.
More *Apprentices* enter; they bring benches, arrange them and

---

11. euch … gelingen: not the warrior, but the singer must win.
17. sel'ger Glut: Genitive absolute. A very vivid manner of expression, of which Wagner makes frequent use in the text. Other instances are *Verlangen, einziger Macht*, p. 105, l. 15; *Friedsam, treuer Sitten*, p. 98, l. 29; *Gleich zwei'n Sonnen, reinster Wonnen*, p. 115, ll. 28 and 29. Nowadays a prepositional construction would be more according to usage.

prepare everything for the session of the *Mastersingers*, all the while talking as follows.

Erster Lehrbube

David, was stehst?

Zweiter Lehrbube

Greif' ans Werk!

Dritter Lehrbube

Hilf uns richten das Gemerk?

David

Zu eifrigst war ich vor euch allen;
schafft nun für euch; hab' ander Gefallen!

Zweiter Lehrbube

5 Was der sich dünkt!

Dritter Lehrbube

Der Lehrling' Muster!

Erster Lehrbube

Das macht, weil sein Meister ein Schuster.

Dritter Lehrbube

Beim Leisten sitzt er mit der Feder.

Zweiter Lehrbube

Beim Dichten mit Draht und Pfriem'.

Erster Lehrbube

Sein' Verse schreibt er auf rotes Leder.

Dritter Lehrbube (with appropriate gestures).

10 Das, dächt' ich, gerbten wir ihm!
(They busy themselves, laughing, with the further arrangements.)

David (after regarding the meditating knight awhile calls out loudly):

"Fanget an!"

Walther (surprised, looks up).

Was soll's?

David (still louder).

"Fanget an!" — So ruft der "Merker;"
nun sollt ihr singen: — wisst ihr das nicht?

Walther

Wer ist der Merker?

David

Wisst ihr das nicht?
War't ihr noch nie bei 'nem Sing-Gericht?

Walther

Noch nie, wo die Richter Handwerker!

David

Seid ihr ein "Dichter?"

Walther

Wär' ich's doch!

David

Waret ihr "Singer?"

Walther

Wüsst' ich's noch?

David

5 Doch "Schulfreund" war't ihr, und "Schüler" zuvor?

Walther

Das klingt mir alles fremd vorm Ohr.

David

Und so grad'hin wollt ihr Meister werden?

Walther

Wie machte das so grosse Beschwerden?

David

O Lene! Lene!

Walther

Wie ihr doch tut!

David

10 O Magdalene!

Walther

Ratet mir gut!

David

Mein Herr! der Singer Meister-Schlag
gewinnt sich nicht in einem Tag.
In Nüremberg der grösste Meister,
    mich lehrt die Kunst Hans Sachs;
15 schon voll ein Jahr mich unterweis't er,

---

3 ff. For the titles **"Dichter,"** **"Singer,"** etc., see Introduction.

dass ich als Schüler wachs'.
Schuhmacherei und Poeterei,
die lern' ich da all einerlei :
hab' ich das Leder glatt geschlagen,
5 lern' ich Vokal und Konsonanz sagen ;
wichst' ich den Draht gar fein und steif,
was sich da reimt, ich wohl begreif';
    den Pfriemen schwingend,
    im Stich die Ahl',
10   was stumpf, was klingend,
    was Mass und Zahl, —
    den Leisten im Schurz —
    was lang, was kurz,
    was hart, was lind,
15   hell oder blind,
    was Waisen, was Milben,
    was Kleb-Silben,
    was Pausen, was Körner,
    Blumen und Dörner,
20 das alles lernt' ich mit Sorg' und Acht :
wie weit nun, meint ihr, dass ich's gebracht?

Walther

Wohl zu 'nem Paar recht guter Schuh'?

David

Ja, dahin hat's noch lange Ruh'!
Ein "Bar" hat manch' Gesätz' und Gebänd';
25 wer da gleich die rechte Regel fänd',
    die richt'ge Naht,
    und den rechten Draht,
    mit gutgefügten "Stollen,"
    den Bar recht zu versohlen.
30 Und dann erst kommt der "Abgesang ;"
dass der nicht kurz, und nicht zu lang,
    und auch keinen Reim enthält,
    der schon im Stollen gestellt. —

10—18. For **stumpf, klingend, Waisen, Pausen, Kleb-Silben,
Körner** consult Introduction as well as Vocabulary.   22—24. David
receives Walter's somewhat ironical answer with perfect seriousness,
evidently mistaking **"Paar"** for **"Bar."**

Wer alles das merkt, weiss und kennt,
wird doch immer noch nicht "Meister" genennt.

Walther

Hilf Gott! Will ich denn Schuster sein? —
In die Singkunst lieber führ' mich ein.

David

5 Ja, hätt' ich's nur selbst erst zum "Singer" gebracht!
Wer glaubt wohl, was das für Mühe macht?
    Der Meister Tön' und Weisen,
    gar viel an Nam' und Zahl,
    die starken und die leisen,
10   wer die wüsste allzumal!
Der "kurze," "lang'" und "überlang'" Ton,
die "Schreibpapier"-, "Schwarz-Dinten"-Weis';
der "rote," "blau'" und "grüne" Ton,
die "Hageblüh"-, "Strohhalm"-, "Fengel"-Weis';
15 der "zarte," der "süsse," der "Rosen"-Ton;
der "kurzen Liebe," der "vergess'ne" Ton;
die "Rosmarin"-, "Gelbveiglein"-Weis';
die "Regenbogen"-, die "Nachtigall"-Weis',
die "englische Zinn"-, die "Zimmtröhren"-Weis',
20 "frisch' Pomeranzen"-, "grün' Lindenblüh"-Weis',
die "Frösch"-, die "Kälber"-, die "Stieglitz"-Weis',
die "abgeschiedene Vielfrass"-Weis';
der "Lerchen"-, der "Schnecken"-, der "Beller"-Ton,
die "Melissenblümlein"-, die "Meiran"-Weis',
25 "Gelblöwenhaut"-, "treu Pelikan"-Weis',
die "buttglänzende Draht"-Weis' . . .

Walther

Hilf Himmel! Welch endlos' Töne-Geleis'!

David

Das sind nur die Namen : nun lernt sie singen,
recht wie die Meister sie gestellt!
30 Jed' Wort und Ton muss klärlich klingen,
wo steigt die Stimm' und wo sie fällt.
Fangt nicht zu hoch, zu tief nicht an,
als es die Stimm' erreichen kann ;
mit dem Atem spart, dass er nicht knappt ;
35 und gar am End' ihr überschnappt.

Vor dem Wort mit der Stimme ja nicht summt,
nach dem Wort mit dem Mund auch nicht brummt;
nicht ändert an "Blum" und "Coloratur,"
jed' Zierrat fest nach des Meisters Spur;
5 verwechselt ihr, würdet gar irr,
verlör't ihr euch, und kämt ins Gewirr: —
        wär' sonst euch alles gelungen,
        da hättet ihr gar "versungen!" —
Trotz grossem Fleiss und Emsigkeit
10 ich selbst noch bracht' es nie so weit.
    So oft ich's versuch' und 's nicht gelingt,
    die "Knieriem-Schlag-Weis" der Meister mir singt:
    wenn dann Jungfer Lene nicht Hülfe weiss,
    sing' ich die "eitel Brot- und Wasser-Weis'!" —
15   Nehmt euch ein Beispiel dran,
        Und lasst von dem Meister-Wahn!
    Denn "Singer" und "Dichter" müsst ihr sein,
    eh' ihr zum "Meister" kehret ein.

Walther

Wer ist nun Dichter?

Lehrbuben (while at work).

                    David! kommst' her?

David

20 Wartet nur, gleich! —
                Wer "Dichter" wär'?
    Habt ihr zum "Singer" euch aufgeschwungen
    und der Meister Töne richtig gesungen,
    füget ihr selbst nun Reim und Wort',
    dass sie genau an Stell' und Ort
25 passten zu einem Meister-Ton,
    dann trüg't ihr den Dichterpreis davon.

Lehrbuben

He, David! Soll man's dem Meister klagen?
Wirst dich bald des Schwatzens entschlagen?

David

Oho! — Ja wohl! Denn helf' ich euch nicht,
30 ohne mich wird alles doch falsch gericht'!

Walther

Nun dies' noch: wer wird "Meister" genannt?

David

Damit, Herr Ritter, ist's so bewandt : —
der Dichter, der aus eig'nem Fleisse
zu Wort' und Reimen, die er erfand,
aus Tönen auch fügt eine neue Weise :
5 der wird als "Meistersinger" erkannt.

Walther (quickly).

So bleibt mir nichts als der Meisterlohn !
Soll ich hier singen,
kann's nur gelingen,
find' ich zum Vers auch den eig'nen Ton.

David (who turns to the *Apprentices*).

10 Was macht ihr denn da ? — Ja, fehl' ich beim Werk
verkehrt nur richtet ihr Stuhl und Gemerk ! —
Ist denn heut' "Singschul'?" — dass ihr's wisst,
das kleine Gemerk ! — nur "Freiung" ist !

The *Apprentices*, who have been arranging to erect a large platform with curtains in the middle of the stage, now put this aside
under *David's* direction, and in its place hastily build a smaller platform of boards. Upon this they place a seat and a little desk before
it, near this a large blackboard, on which they hang a piece of chalk
by a string. The whole is hung with curtains on four sides.

Die Lehrbuben (during their preparations).

Aller End' ist doch David der Allergescheit'st !
15 Nach hohen Ehren gewiss er geizt :
's ist Freiung heut ;
gar sicher er freit,
als vornehmer "Singer" schon er sich spreizt !
Die "Schlag"-reime fest er inne hat,
20 "Arm-Hunger"-Weise singt er glatt ;
die "harte-Tritt"-Weis' doch kennt er am best',
die trat ihm sein Meister hart und fest !
(They laugh.)

David

Ja, lacht nur zu ! Heut' bin ich's nicht ;
ein andrer stellt sich zum Gericht :
25 der war nicht "Schüler," ist nicht "Singer,"
den "Dichter," sagt er, überspring' er ;

12. **dass ihr's wisst:** ironical. 13. **"Freiung":** see Introduction.

denn er ist Junker,
und mit einem Sprung er
denkt ohne weit're Beschwerden,
heut' hier "Meister" zu werden. —
5   D'rum richtet nur fein
das Gemerk dem ein!
Dorthin! — Hierher! — Die Tafel an die Wand,
so dass sie recht dem Merker zur Hand!

         (Turning to *Walther*.)

Ja, ja! — dem "Merker!" — Wird euch wohl bang?
10 Vor ihm schon mancher Werber versang.
Sieben Fehler gibt er euch vor,
      die merkt er mit Kreide dort an;
wer über sieben Fehler verlor,
      hat versungen und ganz vertan!
15   Nun nehmt euch in acht!
      Der Merker wacht.
      Glück auf zum Meistersingen!
Mögt' ihr euch das Kränzlein erschwingen!
Das Blumenkränzlein aus Seiden fein,
20   wird das dem Herrn Ritter beschieden sein?

Die Lehrbuben (who have closed up the Marker's platform,
join hands and dance around it).

"Das Blumenkränzlein aus Seiden fein,
wird das dem Herrn Ritter beschieden sein?"

The arrangements are now completed in the following manner:—
At the right side upholstered chairs are so disposed that they form a
sort of half circle toward the middle. At the end of the chairs, in
the middle of the scene is the Marker's platform, as above de-
scribed. At the left, and opposite the chairs, is the elevated seat, the
"Singstuhl." In the background, near the large curtain, is a long
low bench for the Apprentices. — *Walther*, angry at the taunts of the
boys, has seated himself on the front bench.

Pogner and *Beckmesser*, engaged in conversation, enter from the
sacristy; gradually the other *Masters* assemble. The *Apprentices* re-
tire as soon as the *Masters* begin to appear, and wait respectfully by
the back bench. *David* alone stands at the entrance of the sacristy.

Pogner (to *Beckmesser*).

Seid meiner Treue wohl versehen;
was ich bestimmt, ist euch zu nutz:
25 im Wettgesang müsst ihr bestehen;
wer böte euch als Meister Trutz?

Beckmesser

Doch wollt ihr von dem Punkt nicht weichen,
der mich — ich sag's — bedenklich macht;
kann Evchens Wunsch den Werber streichen,
was nützt mir meine Meister-Pracht?

Pogner

5 Ei sagt! Ich mein', vor allen Dingen
sollt' euch an dem gelegen sein?
Könnt ihr der Tochter Wunsch nicht zwingen
wie möchtet ihr wohl um sie frei'n?

Beckmesser

Ei ja! Gar wohl! D'rum eben bitt' ich,
10 dass bei dem Kind ihr für mich sprecht,
wie ich geworben zart und sittig,
und wie Beckmesser grad euch recht.

Das tu' ich gern.   ### Pogner

Beckmesser (aside).

Er lässt nicht nach!
Wie wehrt' ich da 'nem Ungemach?

Walther (who, when he perceives *Pogner*, rises, goes toward
him, and bows).

15 Gestattet, Meister!

Pogner

Wie! mein Junker!
Ihr sucht mich in der Singschul' hie?
(They greet each other.)

Beckmesser (still to himself).

Verstünden's die Frau'n! Doch schlechtes Geflunker
Gilt ihnen mehr als all' Poesie.

Walther

Hie eben bin ich am rechten Ort.
20 Gesteh' ich's frei, vom Lande fort
Was mich nach Nürnberg trieb,
war nur zur Kunst die Lieb'.
Vergass ich's gestern euch zu sagen,
heut' muss ich's laut zu künden wagen:
25 ein Meistersinger möcht' ich sein.
Schliesst, Meister, in die Zunft mich ein!
(Other *Masters* have entered and advanced.)

Pogner (to those nearest to him).

Kunz Vogelgesang! Freund Nachtigal!
Hört doch, welch' ganz besonderer Fall!
Der Ritter hier, mir wohlbekannt,
hat der Meisterkunst sich zugewandt.
(Greetings.)

Beckmesser (still to himself).

5 Noch such' ich's zu wenden: doch sollt's nicht gelingen,
versuch ich des Mädchens Herz zu ersingen;
in stiller Nacht, von ihr nur gehört.
erfahr' ich, ob auf mein Lied sie schwört.
(Turns.)

Wer ist der Mensch?

Pogner (to *Walther*).

Glaubt, wie mich's freut!
10 Die alte Zeit dünkt mich erneu't.

Beckmesser (still to himself).

Er gefällt mir nicht!

Pogner (continuing).

Was ihr begehrt,
soviel an mir, euch sei's gewährt.

Beckmesser (as before).

Was will der hier? — Wie der Blick ihm lacht!

Pogner (as before).

Half ich euch gern bei des Guts Verkauf,
15 in die Zunft nun nehm' ich euch gleich gern auf.

Beckmesser (as before).

Holla! Sixtus! Auf den hab' acht!

Walther (to *Pogner*).

Habt Dank der Güte
aus tiefstem Gemüte!
Und darf ich denn hoffen,
steht heut' mir noch offen,
20   zu werben um den Preis,
dass ich Meistersinger heiss'?

---

12. **soviel an mir**: *soviel* (*als*) *an mir* (*liegt*). 13. **lacht**: a favorite
word of Wagner, it would seem, for he uses it frequently in all his
dramas.

Beckmesser

Oho ! Fein sacht ! Auf dem Kopf steht kein Kegel !

Pogner

Herr Ritter, dies geh' nun nach der Regel.
Doch heut' ist Freiung : ich schlag' euch vor;
mir leihen die Meister ein willig Ohr.

(The *Mastersingers* have all arrived, *Sachs* last.)

Sachs

Gott grüss' euch, Meister !

Vogelgesang

5   Sind wir beisammen ?

Beckmesser

Der Sachs ist ja da !

Nachtigal

So ruft die Namen !

Fritz Kothner (takes out a list, stands apart and calls
the roll).

Zu einer Freiung und Zunftberatung
ging an die Meister ein' Einladung :
     bei Nenn' und Nam',
10   ob jeder kam,
ruf' ich nun auf, als letzt-entbot'ner,
der ich mich nenn' und bin Fritz Kothner.
Seit ihr da, Veit Pogner ?

Pogner

         Hier zur Hand.

(Seats himself.)

Kothner

Kunz Vogelgesang ?

Vogelgesang

      Ein sich fand.

(Seats himself.)

Kothner

15 Hermann Ortel ?

9. **Nenn'** = *Nennung.*   11. **letzt-entbot'ner :** see Vocab.   **14. sich
fand :** *sich einfinden.*

Ortel

Immer am Ort.
(Seats himself.)

Kothner

Balthasar Zorn?

Zorn

Bleibt niemals fort.
(Seats himself.)

Kothner

Konrad Nachtigal?

Nachtigal

Treu seinem Schlag.
(Seats himself.)

Kothner

Augustin Moser?

Moser

Nie fehlen mag.
(Seats himself.)

Kothner

Niklaus Vogel? — Schweigt?

Ein Lehrbube (springing up from his sea

Ist krank.

Kothner

5 Gut' Bess'rung dem Meister!

Alle Meister

Walt's Gott!

Der Lehrbube

Schön Dank!

(Sits down again.)

Kothner

Hans Sachs?

David (rising officiously.

Da steht er!

Sachs (in threatening tone).

Juckt dich das Fell? —

Verzeiht, Meister! — Sachs ist zur Stell'.
(Seats himself.)

Kothner

Sixtus Beckmesser?

Beckmesser

Immer bei Sachs,
dass den Reim ich lern' von "blüh' und wachs'."

(Takes a seat near *Sachs*, who laughs.)

Kothner

Ulrich Eisslinger?

Eisslinger

Hier!
(Seats himself.)

Kothner

Hans Foltz?

Foltz

Bin da.

(Seats himself.)

Kothner

Hans Schwarz?

Schwarz

Zuletzt: Gott wollt's!
(Seats himself.)

Kothner

5 Zur Sitzung gut und voll die Zahl.
Beliebt's, wir schreiten zur Merkerwahl?

Vogelgesang

Wohl eh'r nach dem Fest.

Beckmesser (to *Kothner*).

Pressiert's den Herrn!
Mein Stell' und Amt lass' ich ihm gern.

Pogner

Nicht doch, ihr Meister! Lasst das jetzt fort.
10 Für wicht'gen Antrag bitt' ich ums Wort.

(All the *Masters* rise, and then seat themselves again.)

Kothner

Das habt ihr, Meister! Sprecht!

Pogner

Nun hört, und versteht mich recht! —
Das schöne Fest, Johannis-Tag,
    ihr wisst, begeh'n wir morgen:
auf grüner Au', am Blumenhag,
bei Spiel und Tanz im Lustgelag,
    an froher Brust geborgen,
    vergessen seiner Sorgen,
ein jeder freut sich, wie er mag.
Die Singschul' ernst im Kirchenchor
    die Meister selbst vertauschen;
mit Kling und Klang hinaus zum Tor,
auf off'ne Wiese ziehn sie vor,
    bei hellen Festes Rauschen;
    das Volk sie lassen lauschen
dem Frei-Gesang mit Laien-Ohr,
Zu einem Werb'- und Wett-Gesang
    gestellt sind Siegespreise,
und beide rühmt man weit und lang,
    die Gabe wie die Weise.
Nun schuf mich Gott zum reichen Mann;
Und gibt ein jeder, wie er kann,
    so musst' ich fleissig sinnen,
    was ich gäb' zu gewinnen,
    dass ich nicht käm' zu Schand':
so höret, was ich fand. —
In deutschen Landen viel gereis't,
    hat oft es mich verdrossen,
dass man den Bürger wenig preis't,
    ihn karg nennt und verschlossen:
an Höfen, wie an nied'rer Statt,
des bitt'ren Tadels ward ich satt,
    dass nur auf Schacher und Geld
    sein Merk' der Bürger stellt'.
Dass wir im weiten deutschen Reich
    die Kunst einzig noch pflegen,
    d'ran dünkt' ihnen wenig gelegen:
doch wie uns das zur Ehre gereich',
    und dass mit hohem Mut

36. **dran dünkt':** see *dünken* and *gelegen.*

wir schätzen, was schön und gut,
was wert die Kunst, und was sie gilt,
das ward ich der Welt zu zeigen gewillt.
D'rum hört, Meister, die Gab',
5   die als Preis bestimmt ich hab';
dem Singer, der im Kunst-Gesang
vor allem Volk den Preis errang
    am Sankt Johannistag,
    sei er, wer er auch mag,
10 dem geb' ich, ein Kunst-gewog'ner,
von Nürenberg Veit Pogner,
mit all' meinem Gut, wie's geh' und steh'
Eva, mein einzig Kind, zur Eh'.

Die Meister (to one another, animatedly).

Das nenn' ich ein Wort !   Ein Wort, ein **Mann** !
15 Da sieht man, was ein Nürnberger kann !
D'rob preis't man euch noch weit und breit,
den wack'ren Bürger Pogner Veit !

Die Lehrbuben (gaily jumping up).

Alle Zeit, weit und breit :
    Pogner Veit !

Vogelgesang

20 Wer möchte da nicht ledig sein !

Sachs

Sein Weib gäb' gern wohl mancher d'rein !

Kothner

Auf, ledig' Mann !
Jetzt macht euch 'ran !

Pogner

Nun hört noch, wie ich's ernstlich mein' !
25 Ein' leblos' Gabe stell' ich nicht :
ein Mägdlein sitzt mit zu Gericht.
Den Preis erkennt die Meister-Zunft ;
doch gilt's der Eh', so will's Vernunft,
    dass ob der Meister Rat
30   die Braut den Ausschlag hat.

3. **gewillt** = (*gewillet*) and *gewollt*.

Beckmesser (to *Kothner*).

Dünkt euch das klug?

Kothner (aloud).

Versteh' ich gut,
ihr gebt uns in des Mägdleins Hut?

Beckmesser

Gefährlich das!

Kothner

Stimmt es nicht bei,
wie wäre dann der Meister Urteil frei?

Beckmesser

5 Lasst's gleich wählen nach Herzens Ziel,
und lasst den Meistergesang aus dem Spiel!

Pogner

Nicht so! Wie doch? Versteht mich recht!
Wem ihr Meister den Preis zusprecht,
die Maid kann dem verwehren,
10   doch nie einen andren begehren:
ein Meistersinger muss er sein;
nur wen ihr krönt, den soll sie frei'n.

Sachs

Verzeiht!
Vielleicht schon ginget ihr zu weit.
15 Ein Mädchenherz und Meisterkunst
erglühn nicht stets von gleicher Brunst;
der Frauen Sinn, gar unbelehrt,
dünkt mich dem Sinn des Volks gleich wert.
Wollt ihr nun vor dem Volke zeigen,
20   wie hoch die Kunst ihr ehrt;
und lasst ihr dem Kind die Wahl zu eigen,
wollt nicht, dass dem Spruch es wehrt':
so lasst das Volk auch Richter sein;
mit dem Kinde sicher stimmt's überein.

Die Meister (uneasily, one to the other).

25 Oho! Das Volk? Ja, das wäre schön!
Ade dann Kunst und Meistertön'!

Kothner

Nein, Sachs! Gewiss, das hat keinen Sinn!
Gäb't ihr dem Volk die Regeln hin?

Sachs

Vernehmt mich recht !   Wie ihr doch tut !
Gesteht, ich kenn' die Regeln gut ;
und dass die Zunft die Regeln bewahr',
bemüh' ich mich selbst schon manches Jahr.
5 Doch einmal im Jahre fänd' ich's weise,
dass man die Regeln selbst probier',
ob in der Gewohnheit trägem G'leise
ihr' Kraft und Leben sich nicht verlier' :
    und ob ihr der Natur
10   noch seid auf rechter Spur,
      das sagt euch nur,
wer nichts weiss von der Tabulatur.

      (The *Apprentices* jump up and rub their hands.)

Beckmesser

Hei ! wie sich die Buben freuen !

Sachs (continuing earnestly).

D'rum mocht's euch nie gereuen,
15 dass jährlich am Sankt Johannisfest,
statt dass das Volk man kommen lässt,
herab aus hoher Meister-Wolk'
ihr selbst euch wendet zu dem Volk'.
    Dem Volke wollt ihr behagen ;
20   nun dächt' ich, läg' es nah',
    ihr liesst es selbst euch auch sagen,
    ob das ihm zur Lust geschah.
Dass Volk und Kunst gleich blüh' und wachs',
bestellt ihr so, mein' ich, Hans Sachs.

Vogelgesang

25 Ihr meint's wohl recht !

Kothner

      Doch steht's drum faul.

Nachtigal

Wenn spricht das Volk, halt' ich das Maul.

Kothner

Der Kunst droht' allweil' Fall und Schmach,
läuft sie der Gunst des Volkes nach.

Beckmesser

D'rin bracht' er's weit, der hier so dreist:
Gassenhauer dichtet er meist.

Pogner

Freund Sachs, was ich mein', ist schon neu:
zuviel auf einmal brächte Reu'! —
5 So frag' ich, ob den Meistern gefällt
Gab' und Regel, wie ich's gestellt?
(The *Masters* rise.)

Sachs

Mir genügt der Jungfer Ausschlag-Stimm'.

Beckmesser (aside).

Der Schuster weckt doch stets mir Grimm!

Kothner

Wer schreibt sich als Werber ein?
10   Ein Jung-Gesell muss es sein.

Beckmesser

Vielleicht auch ein Witwer?   Fragt nur den Sachs!

Sachs

Nicht doch, Herr Merker!   Aus jüng'rem Wachs
als ich und ihr muss der Freier sein,
soll Evchen ihm den Preis verleih'n.

Beckmesser

15 Als wie auch ich? — Grober Gesell!

Kothner

Begehrt wer Freiung, der komm' zur Stell'!
Ist jemand gemeld't, der Freiung begehrt?

Pogner

Wohl, Meister!   Zur Tagesordnung kehrt!
Und nehmt von mir Bericht,
20   wie ich auf Meister-Pflicht
einen jungen Ritter empfehle,
der wünscht, dass man ihn wähle,

---

11. **Witwer** = Hans Sachs.   One of the finest touches in the whole
work is the half lover-like, half fatherly, but always self-denying love
of Hans Sachs for Eva.

und heut' als Meistersinger frei'. —
Mein Junker von Stolzing, kommt herbei!

Walther (steps forward and bows).

Beckmesser (aside)

Dacht' ich mir's doch! Geht's da hinaus, Veit?
(Aloud.)
Meister, ich mein', zu spät ist's der Zeit.

Die Meister (to one another).

5 Der Fall ist neu. — Ein Ritter gar?
Soll man sich freu'n? — Oder wär' Gefahr?
Immerhin hat's ein gross' Gewicht,
dass Meister Pogner für ihn spricht.

Kothner

Soll uns der Junker willkommen sein,
10 zuvor muss er wohl vernommen sein.

Pogner

Vernehmt ihn gut! Wünsch' ich ihm Glück,
nicht bleib' ich doch hinter der Regel zurück.
Tut, Meister, die Fragen!

Kothner

So mög' uns der Junker sagen:
15 ist er frei und ehrlich geboren?

Pogner

Die Frage gebt verloren,
da ich euch selbst dess' Bürge steh',
dass er aus frei und edler Eh':
von Stolzing Walther aus Frankenland,
20 nach Brief' und Urkund' mir wohlbekannt.
Als seines Stammes letzter Spross,
verliess er neulich Hof und Schloss,
und zog nach Nürnberg her,
dass er hier Bürger wär'.

Beckmesser (to his neighbor).

25 Neu Junker-Unkraut! Tut nicht gut.

1. frei' = *freien*. 3. Geht's da hinaus: see Vocab. (*hinaus*). 4. der
Zeit: Genitive. 16. gebt verloren: see *geben*.

Nachtigal (aloud).

Freund Pogners Wort Genüge tut.

Sachs

Wie längst von den Meistern beschlossen ist,
ob Herr, ob Bauer, hier nichts beschiesst:
hier fragt sich's nach der Kunst allein,
5 wer will ein Meistersinger sein.

Kothner

Drum nun frag' ich zur Stell';
welch' Meister's seid ihr Gesell'?

Walther

Am stillen Herd in Winterszeit,
wenn Burg und Hof mir eingeschnei't,
10 wie einst der Lenz so lieblich lacht',
und wie er bald wohl neu erwacht',
ein altes Buch, vom Ahn' vermacht,
    gab das mir oft zu lesen;
Herr Walther von der Vogelweid',
15   der ist mein Meister gewesen.

Sachs

Ein guter Meister!

Beckmesser

            Doch lang' schon tot:
wie lehrt' ihn der wohl der Regel Gebot?

Kothner

Doch in welcher Schul' das Singen
mocht' euch zu lernen gelingen?

Walther

20 Wann dann die Flur vom Frost befreit,
und wiederkehrt die Sommerszeit,
was einst in langer Winternacht
das alte Buch mir kund gemacht,
das schallte laut in Waldespracht,
25   das hört' ich hell erklingen:

---

14. **Herr ... Vogelweid':** the same character appears in Wagner's
Tannhäuser. Many other poets have also made use of him. He was
a real character, a Minnesinger, and took part in the famous song-
contest held at the Wartburg in 1207 under the patronage of Landgraf
Hermann of Thüringen.

im Wald dort auf der Vogelweid',
   da lernt' ich auch das Singen.

Beckmesser

Oho! Von Finken und Meisen
   lerntet ihr Meister-Weisen?
5 Das mag denn wohl auch darnach sein!

Vogelgesang

Zwei art'ge Stollen fasst' er da ein.

Beckmesser

Ihr lobt ihn, Meister Vogelgesang?
Wohl weil er vom Vogel lernt' den Gesang?

Kothner (aside, to the *Masters*).

Was meint ihr, Meister? Frag' ich noch fort?
10 Mich dünkt, der Junker ist fehl am Ort.

Sachs

Das wird sich bäldlich zeigen:
   wenn rechte Kunst ihm eigen,
   und gut er sie bewährt,
   was gilt's, wer sie ihn gelehrt?

Kothner

15 Meint, Junker, ihr in Sang' und Dicht'
   euch rechtlich unterwiesen,
und wollt ihr, dass im Zunftgericht
   zum Meister wir euch kiesen:
seid ihr bereit, ob euch geriet
20 mit neuer Find' ein Meisterlied,
   nach Dicht' und Weis' eu'r eigen,
   zur Stunde jetzt zu zeigen?

Walther

Was Winternacht,
   was Waldes Pracht,
25   was Buch und Hain mich wiesen;
was Dichter-Sanges Wundermacht
   mir heimlich wollt' erschliessen;
   was Rosses Schritt
   beim Waffen-Ritt,

---

5. **darnach:** see Vocab.   10. **fehl:** see Vocab.   19. **geriet** = *ge-lingen*.   20. **Find'** = *Findung*.

was Reihen-Tanz
bei heit'rem Schanz
mir sinnend gab zu lauschen:
gilt es des Lebens höchsten Preis
5   um Sang mir einzutauschen,
zu eig'nem Wort und eig'ner Weis'
will einig mir es fliessen,
als Meistersang, ob den ich weiss,
euch Meistern sich ergiessen.

Beckmesser
10 Entnahmt ihr 'was der Worte Schwall?

Vogelgesang
Ei nun, er wagt's!

Nachtigal
·   Merkwürd'ger Fall!

Kothner
Nun, Meister, wenn's gefällt,
werd' das Gemerk bestellt. —
Wählt der Herr einen heil'gen Stoff?

Walther
15   Was heilig mir,
der Liebe Panier
schwing' und sing' ich, mir zu Hoff'.

Kothner
Das gilt uns weltlich.   Drum allein,
Merker Beckmesser, schliesst euch ein!

Beckmesser (rising and walking toward the Marker's box).
20 Ein sau'res Amt, und heut' zumal;
wohl gibt's mit der Kreide manche Qual. —
Herr Ritter, wisst:
Sixtus Beckmesser Merker ist;
hier im Gemerk
25 verrichtet er still sein strenges Werk.
Sieben Fehler gibt er euch vor,
die merkt er mit Kreide dort an:
wenn er über sieben Fehler verlor,

3. **mir sinnend,** etc.: see *lauschen.*   17. **Hoff'** = *Hoffnung.*

.dann versang der Herr Rittersmann. —
    Gar fein er hört ;
doch dass er euch den Mut nicht stört,
    säh't ihr ihm zu,
5   so gibt er euch Ruh,
und schliesst sich gar hier ein, —
lässt Gott euch befohlen sein.

He seats himself within and then with his last words stretches his
head out and, after a scornfully familiar nod, draws the curtains,
which the *Apprentices* have opened for him, together, so that he becomes invisible.

Kothner (takes down the *Leges Tabulaturae*, which the
Apprentices have hung on the wall).

Was euch zum Liede Richt' und Schnur,
vernehmt nun aus der Tabulatur. —
    (He reads.)
10 "Ein jedes Meistergesanges Bar
stell' ordentlich ein Gemässe dar
aus unterschiedlichen Gesetzen,
die Keiner soll verletzen.
Ein Gesetz besteht aus zweenen Stollen,
15 die gleiche Melodei haben sollen ;
Der Stoll' aus etlicher Vers' Gebänd'.
der Vers hat seinen Reim am End'.
Darauf so folgt der Abgesang,
der sei auch etlich' Verse lang,
20 und hab' sein' besondere Melodei,
als nicht im Stollen zu finden sei.
Derlei Gemässes mehre Baren
soll ein jed' Meisterlied bewahren ;
und wer ein neues Lied gericht',
25 das über vier der Silben nicht
eingreift in andrer Meister Weis',
des' Lied erwerb' sich Meister-Preis."
Nun setzt euch in den Singestuhl !

Walther

Hier in den Stuhl ?

Kothner

    Wie's Brauch der Schul'.

12. **Gesetzen** = *Gesätze.*

Walther (mounts the chair and seats himself, ill-pleased).

Für dich, Geliebte, sei's getan?

Kothner (very loud).

Der Sänger sitzt.

Beckmesser (from his concealment, very harshly).

Fanget an!

Walther (after a pause to collect himself).

Fanget an?
So rief der Lenz in den Wald,
5   dass laut es ihn durchhallt;
und wie in ferneren Wellen
der Hall von dannen flieht,
von weither nah't ein Schwellen,
das mächtig näher zieht;
10   es schwillt und schallt,
es tönt der Wald
von holder Stimmen Gemenge;
nun laut und hell
schon nah' zur Stell',
15   wie wächst der Schwall?
Wie Glockenhall
ertos't des Jubels Gedränge?
Der Wald,
wie bald
20   antwortet er dem Ruf
der neu ihm Leben schuf,
stimmte an
das süsse Lenzes-Lied?

(Repeated and discouraging sighs from the Marker are heard,
together with violent scratching strokes of the chalk on the slate.
Walther notices it, and is disturbed for a moment, but continues.)

In einer Dornenhecken,
25   von Neid und Gram verzehrt,
muss' er sich da verstecken,
der Winter, Grimm-bewehrt;
von dürrem Laub umrauscht
er lauert da und lauscht,
30   wie er das frohe Singen
zu Schaden könnte bringen. —

(Rising displeased from his chair.)

Doch : fanget an !
So rief es mir in die Brust,
als noch ich von Liebe nicht wusst'.
Da fühlt' ich's tief sich regen,
5 als weckt' es mich aus dem Traum ;
mein Herz mit bebenden Schlägen
erfüllte des Busens Raum :
das Blut, es wall't
mit Allgewalt,
10 geschwellt von neuem Gefühle ;
aus warmer Nacht
mit Übermacht
schwillt mir zum Meer
der Seufzer Heer
15 in wildem Wonne-Gewühle :
die Brust,
mit Lust
antwortet sie dem Ruf,
der neu ihr Leben schuf :
20 stimmt nun an
das hehre Liebes-Lied !

Beckmesser (who has grown more and more restive, tears open the curtains).

Seid ihr nun fertig ?

Walther

Wie fraget ihr ?

Beckmesser (holding up the slate completely covered with chalk marks).

Mit der Tafel ward ich fertig schier.

(The *Masters* are forced to laugh.)

Walther

Hört doch ! Zu meiner Frauen Preis
25 gelang ich jetzt erst mit der Weis'.

Beckmesser (leaving his box).

Singt, wo ihr wollt ! Hier habt ihr vertan. —
Ihr Meister, schaut die Tafel euch an :
so lang' ich leb', ward's nicht erhört ;
ich glaubt's nicht, wenn ihr's all' auch schwört ?

(The *Masters* seem in great commotion.)

Walther

Erlaubt ihr's Meister, dass er mich stört?
Blieb'ich von allen ungehört?

Pogner

Ein Wort, Herr Merker! Ihr seid gereizt!

Beckmesser

Sei Merker fortan, wer darnach geizt!
5 Doch dass der Ritter versungen hat,
beleg' ich erst noch vor der Meister Rat.
Zwar wird's 'ne harte Arbeit sein:
wo beginnen, da wo nicht aus noch ein?
Von falscher Zahl, und falschem Gebänd'
10   schweig' ich schon ganz und gar;
zu kurz, zu lang, wer ein End' da fänd'!
    Wer meint hier im Ernst einen Bar?
Auf "blinde Meinung" klag' ich allein:
sagt, konnt' ein Sinn unsinniger sein?

Mehrere Meister

15 Man ward nicht klug! Ich muss gestehn,
Ein Ende konnte keiner erseh'n.

Beckmesser

Und dann die Weis'! Welch tolles Gekreis'
aus "Abenteuer-", "blau Rittersporn"-Weis',
"hoch Tannen"- und "stolz Jüngling"-Ton!

Kothner

20 Ja, ich verstand gar nichts davon!

Beckmesser

Kein Absatz wo, kein' Coloratur,
von Melodei auch nicht eine Spur!

Mehrere Meister (to one another).

Wer nennt das Gesang?
's ward einem bang!
25 Eitel Ohrgeschinder!
Gar nichts dahinter!

Kothner

Und gar vom Singstuhl ist er gesprungen!

---

8. da ... ein = *kein Anfang, kein Ende.* 24. bang. see VOCAB.

Beckmesser

Wird erst auf die Fehlerprobe gedrungen?
Oder gle:ch erklärt, dass er versungen?

Sachs (who from the beginning had listened to *Walther* with increasing interest).

Halt! Meister! Nicht so geeilt!
Nicht jeder eure Meinung teilt. —
5   Des Ritters Lied und Weise,
sie fand ich neu, doch nicht verwirrt;
     verliess er uns're G'leise,
schritt er doch fest und unbeirrt.
     Wollt ihr nach Regeln messen,
10 was nicht nach eurer Regeln Lauf,
     der eig'nen Spur vergessen,
sucht davon erst die Regeln auf!

Beckmesser

Aha! Schon recht! Nun hört ihr's doch:
den Stümpern öffnet Sachs ein Loch,
15   da aus und ein nach Belieben
     ihr Wesen leicht sie trieben.
Singet dem Volk auf Markt und Gassen;
hier wird nach den Regeln nur eingelassen!

Sachs

Herr Merker, was doch solch ein Eifer?
20   Was doch so wenig Ruh'?
Eu'r Urteil, dünkt mich, wäre reifer,
     hörtet ihr besser zu.
Darum, so komm' ich jetzt zum Schluss,
dass den Junker zu End' man hören muss.

Beckmesser

25 Der Meister Zunft, die ganze Schul',
gegen den Sachs da sind wie Null.

Sachs

Verhüt' es Gott, was ich begehr',
dass das nicht nach den Gesetzen wär'!
     Doch da nun steht's geschrieben,
30 der Merker werde so bestellt,
     dass weder Hass noch Lieben
das Urteil trüben, das er fällt.

Geht der nun gar auf Freiers-Füssen,
wie sollt' er da die Lust nicht büssen,
den Nebenbuhler auf dem Stuhl
zu schmähen vor der ganzen Schul'?

(*Walther*, in sudden anger.)

Nachtigal

Ihr geht zu weit!

Kothner

Persönlichkeit!

5

Pogner (to the *Masters*).

Vermeidet, Meister, Zwist und Streit!

Beckmesser

Ei, was kümmert's doch Meister Sachsen,
  auf was für Füssen ich geh'?
Liess' er d'rob lieber Sorge sich wachsen,
10   dass nichts mir drück' die Zeh'!
Doch seit mein Schuster ein grosser Poet,
gar übel es um mein Schuhwerk steht;
    da seht, wie er schlappt,
    und überall klappt!
15   All' seine Vers' und Reim'
    liess' ich ihm gern daheim,
Historien, Spiel' und Schwänke dazu,
brächt er mir morgen die neuen Schuh'!

Sachs

  Ihr mahnt mich da gar recht:
20   doch schickt sich's, Meister, sprecht,
dass, find' ich selbst dem Eseltreiber
  ein Sprüchlein auf die Sohl',
dem hochgelahrten Herrn Stadtschreiber
  ich nichts draufschreiben soll?
25 Das Sprüchlein, das eu'r würdig sei,
mit all' meiner armen Poeterei
  fand ich noch nicht zur Stund';
  doch wird's wohl jetzt mir kund,
wenn ich des Ritters Lied gehört: —
30 drum sing' er nun weiter ungestört!

(*Walther*, in great excitement, remounts the singer's chair.)

Beckmesser

Nichts weiter! Zum Schluss!

Die Meister

           Genug! Zum Schluss!

Sachs (to *Walther*).

Singt, dem Herrn Merker zum Verdruss!

Beckmesser

(as *Walther* begins, fetches the slate from the Marker's box, and, during the following, holds it up before the *Masters*, first to one and then the other, whom he at last gathers into a circle about him, and continues to exhibit the slate).

    Was sollte man da noch hören?
    Wär's nicht nur uns zu betören?
5   Jeden der Fehler gross und klein,
    seht genau auf der Tafel ein. —
    "Falsch Gebänd," "unredbare Worte,"
    "Kleb-Sylben," hier "Laster" gar;
    "Äquivoca," "Reim am falschen Orte,"
10 "verkehrt," "verstellt" der ganze Bar;
    ein "Flickgesang" hier zwischen den Stollen;
    "blinde Meinung" allüberall;
    "unklare Wort'," "Differenz," hie "Schrollen,"
    da "falscher Atem," hier "Überfall."
15 Ganz unverständliche Melodei!
    Aus allen Tönen ein Mischgebräu'!
    Scheu'tet ihr nicht das Ungemach,
    Meister, zählt mir die Striche nach!
    Verloren hätt' er schon mit dem acht':
20 doch soweit wie der hat's noch keiner gebracht!
    Wohl über fünfzig, schlecht gezählt!
    Sagt, ob ihr euch den zum Meister wählt?

Die Meister (to one another).

    Ja wohl, so ist's! Ich seh' es recht!
    Mit dem Herrn Ritter steht es schlecht.
25 Mag Sachs von ihm halten, was er will,
    hier in der Singschul' schweig' er still!
    Bleibt einem jeden doch unbenommen,
        wen er zum Genossen begehrt?
    Wär' uns der erste Best' willkommen,

was blieben die Meister dann wert? —
Hei! Wie sich der Ritter da quält!
Der Sachs hat ihn sich erwählt! —
's ist ärgerlich gar! D'rum macht ein End'!
Auf, Meister, stimmt und erhebt die Händ'!

Pogner (aside).

Ja wohl, ich seh's, was mir nicht recht:
mit meinem Junker steht es schlecht!
Weiche ich hier der Übermacht,
mir ahnet, dass mir's Sorge macht.
Wie gerne säh' ich ihn angenommen,
als Eidam wär' er mir gar wert;
nenn' ich den Sieger nun willkommen,
wer weiss, ob ihn mein Kind begehrt!
    Gesteh' ich's, dass mich das quält,
    ob Eva den Meister wählt!

Walther
(in wild and desperate enthusiasm, standing erect in the singer's chair and looking down on the commotion of the *Masters*).

Aus finst'rer Dornenhecken
Die Eule rauscht' hervor,
tät rings mit Kreischen wecken
der Raben heis'ren Chor:
in nächt'gem Heer zu Hauf
wie krächzen all' da auf,
mit ihren Stimmen, den hohlen,
die Elstern, Kräh'n und Dohlen!
    Auf da steigt
mit gold'nem Flügelpaar
ein Vogel wunderbar:
sein strahlend hell Gefieder
licht in den Lüften blinkt;
schwebt selig hin und wieder,
zu Flug und Flucht mir winkt.
    Es schwillt das Herz
    von süssem Schmerz,
der Not entwachsen Flügel;
    es schwingt sich auf

---

18. **tät:** see *tun*.

zum kühnen Lauf,
zum Flug durch die Luft
aus der Städte Gruft,
dahin zum heim'schen Hügel ;
5 dahin zur grünen Vogelweid',
wo Meister Walther einst mich freit';
da sing' ich hell und hehr
der liebsten Frauen Ehr':
auf da steigt,
10 ob Meister-Kräh'n ihm ungeneigt,
das stolze Minne-Lied. —
Ade ! ihr Meister, hienied' !

(With a gesture full of pride and contempt, he leaves the chair
and turns away to go.)

Sachs (following *Walther's* song).

Ha, welch ein Mut !
Begeist'rungs-Glut ! —
15 Ihr Meister, schweigt doch und hört !
Hört, wenn Sachs euch beschwört ! —
Herr Merker da ! gönnt doch nur Ruh' !
Lasst and're hören ! gebt das nur zu ! —
Umsonst ! All eitel Trachten !
20 Kaum vernimmt man sein eigen Wort !
Des Junkers will keiner achten : —
das heiss' ich Mut, singt der noch fort !
Das Herz auf dem rechten Fleck :
ein wahrer Dichter-Reck' ! —
25 Mach' ich, Hans Sachs, wohl Vers' und Schuh',
ist Ritter der und Poet dazu.

Die Lehrbuben

(who all along have been rubbing their hands with glee and springing up from their seats, now, toward the end, join hands and
dance around the Marker's platform).

Glück auf zum Meistersingen,
mögt' ihr euch das Kränzlein erschwingen !
Das Blumenkränzlein aus Seiden fein,
30 wird das dem Herrn Ritter beschieden sein ?

Beckmesser

Nun, Meister, kündet's an !

(The majority hold up their hands.)

24. **Dichter-Reck'** : see *Recke*.

Alle Meister

Versungen und vertan!

Confusion everywhere. The *Apprentices* in merry tumult take possession of the platform and Masters' benches, whereby much confusion and disorder is caused among the Masters who are striving to pass through the exit. *Sachs*, who alone has remained in the foreground, looks thoughtfully at the empty singing-chair. When the *Apprentices* remove it, *Sachs* turns away with a discouraged but humorous gesture and then the curtain falls.

ZWEITER AUFZUG

The front of the stage is a longitudinal section of a street, which is intersected in the middle by a narrow alley, winding crookedly toward the back, so that in the front center of the stage are two corner houses, of which one, a stately dwelling on the right, is *Pogner's*, the other, simpler, is that of *Sachs*. A flight of several steps leads from the front street to *Pogner's* house; there are sunken doors and on either side of the passage stone seats. Near to *Pogner's* house, on the right, is a sturdy linden, with green shrubbery at its base, surrounding a stone seat. The entrance to *Sachs's* house is also on the street; a door, divided crosswise, leads directly into his workshop. Two windows, one belonging to the workshop and the other to an inner chamber, open on to the alley. (All the houses in both street and alley must be available for stage action.)

A pleasant summer evening; during the first scene night gradually approaches.

David is closing the shutters toward the alley on the outside. Other *Apprentices* are doing the same for the other houses.

Lehrbuben (while at work).

Johannistag! Johannistag!
Blumen und Bänder so viel man mag!

David (aside).

"Das Blumenkränzlein von Seiden fein,
möcht' es mir balde beschieden sein!"

Magdalene

(coming out of *Pogner's* house with a basket on her arm, seeks to approach *David* unperceived).

Bst! David!

David (turning toward the alley).

Ruft ihr schon wieder?
Singt allein eure dummen Lieder!

Lehrbuben

David, was soll's?
Wär'st nicht so stolz,
schaut'st besser um,
5   wär'st nicht so dumm!
"Johannistag! Johannistag!"
Wie der nur die Jungfer Lene nicht kennen mag!

Magdalene

David! hör' doch! kehr' dich zu mir!

David

Ach, Jungfer Lene! Ihr seid hier?

Magdalene (pointing to her basket).

10 Bring' dir was Gut's; schau' nur hinein!
Das soll für mein lieb' Schätzel sein. —
Erst aber schnell, wie ging's mit dem Ritter?
Du rietest ihm gut? Er gewann den Kranz?

David

Ach, Jungfer Lene! Da steht's bitter;
15 der hat vertan und versungen ganz!

Magdalene

Versungen? Vertan?

David

Was geht's euch nur an?

Magdalene

(quickly snatching away the basket for which *David* stretches out his
hand).

Hand von der Taschen!
Nichts da zu naschen! —
Hilf Gott! Unser Junker vertan!

(She goes back into the house with a gesture of despair.)

David (looks after her dumfounded).

14. **Da steht's bitter**: see *stehen.*

Die Lehrbuben

(who have crept up unnoticed and listened, and now come up to *David*
as if congratulating him).

Heil, Heil zur Eh' dem jungen Mann!
Wie glücklich hat er gefreit!
Wir hörten's all', und sahen's an:
der er sein Herz geweiht,
für die er lässt sein Leben,
die hat ihm den Korb nicht gegeben.

David (starting up).

Was steht ihr hier faul?
Gleich haltet eu'r Maul!

Die Lehrbuben (dancing about *David*).

Johannistag! Johannistag!
Da freit' ein jeder wie er mag.
Der Meister freit!
der Bursche freit,
Da gibt's Geschlamb' und Geschlumbfer!
Der Alte freit
die junge Maid,
der Bursche die alte Jumbfer! —
Juchhei! Juchhei! Johannistag!

David, in his rage, is on the point of flying at the boys, when
Sachs, who has come down the alley, steps between them. The boys
scatter.

Sachs

Was gibt's? Treff' ich dich wieder am Schlag?

David

Nicht ich! Schandlieder singen die.

Sachs

Hör' nicht drauf! Lern's besser wie sie! —
Zur Ruh'! ins Haus! Schliess' und mach' Licht!

David

Hab' ich noch Singstund'?

Sachs

Nein, singst nicht!

---

6. **die hat...gegeben.** A play on the figurative and literal meaning of the phrase. See *Korb*. 13. **Da gibt's...:** see *Geschlamb'*.
16. **Jumbfer** = *Jungfer.*

Zur Straf' für dein heutig' frech' Erdreisten. —
Die neuen Schuh' steck' auf den Leisten!

Both go into the workshop and disappear through an inner door.
The *Apprentices*, too, have dispersed.

Pogner and *Eva*, as if returning from a walk, come silently down
the alley, lost in thought, the daughter leaning lightly on the father's
arm.

Pogner

(still in the alley, peeping through a chink in the shutters into *Sachs's*
workshop).

Lass sehn, ob Nachbar Sachs zu Haus? —
Gern spräch' ich ihn. Trät' ich wohl ein?

(*David* comes out of the chamber with a light, seats himself at the
work-table by the window and begins to work.)

Eva

5 Er scheint daheim : kommt Licht heraus.

Pogner

Tu ich's? — Zu was doch? — Besser, nein!
(Turns away.)
Will einer Selt'nes wagen,
was liess' er da sich sagen? — —
(After some reflection.)
War er's nicht, der meint', ich ging zu weit? . . .
10 Und blieb ich nicht im Geleise,
war's nicht in seiner Weise? —
Doch war's vielleicht auch — Eitelkeit? —
(To Eva.)
Und du, mein Kind, du sagst mir nichts?

Eva

Ein folgsam Kind, gefragt nur spricht's.

Pogner

15 Wie klug! Wie gut! — Komm', setz' dich hier
ein' Weil' noch auf die Bank zu mir.
(Seats himself on the stone seat under the linden.)

Eva

Wird's nicht zu kühl?
's war heut gar schwül.

3. **sehn** = *sehen*. 9. Refers to Pogner's offer before the masters,
and Sachs's suggested alteration of the same, p. 40, ll. 14—24.

Pogner

Nicht doch, 's ist mild und labend;
gar lieblich lind der Abend.

(*Eva* seats herself somewhat nervously.)

Das deutet auf den schönsten Tag,
der morgen dir soll scheinen.
5 O Kind, sagt dir kein Herzensschlag,
welch' Glück dich morgen treffen mag,
wenn Nürenberg, die ganze Stadt
mit Bürgern und Gemeinen,
mit Zünften, Volk und hohem Rat,
10   vor dir sich soll vereinen,
dass du den Preis,
das edle Reis,
erteilest als Gemahl
dem Meister deiner Wahl?

Eva

15 Lieb' Vater, muss es ein Meister sein?

Pogner

Hör' wohl : ein Meister deiner Wahl.

(*Magdalene* appears at the door and beckons to *Eva*.)

Eva (absent-mindedly).

Ja, — meiner Wahl. — Doch, tritt nun ein —
Gleich, Lene, gleich! — zum Abendmahl.

Pogner (with vexation, getting up).

's gibt doch keinen Gast?

Eva (as before).

Wohl den Junker?

Pogner (surprised).

Wie so?

Eva

20 Sahst ihn heut' nicht?

Pogner (half aside).

Ward sein nicht froh. —
Nicht doch! — Was denn? — Ei! werd ich dumm?

Eva

Lieb Väterchen, komm'! Geh', kleid' dich um!

20. **sein'** = genitive.

Pogner (going ahead into the house).

Hm! — Was geht mir im Kopf doch 'rum?
(Exit.)

Magdalene (cautiously).

Hast was heraus?

Eva (likewise).

Bleib still und stumm.

Magdalene

Sprach David: meint', er habe vertan.

Eva.

Der Ritter! — Hilf Gott, was fing' ich an?
5 Ach, Lene, die Angst! Wo 'was erfahren?

Magdalene

Vielleicht vom Sachs?

Eva

　　　　　Ach, der hat mich lieb!
Gewiss, ich geh' hin.

Magdalene

　　　　　Lass drin nichts gewahren!
Der Vater merkt' es, wenn man jetzt blieb'. —
Nach dem Mahl: dann hab' ich dir noch 'was zu sagen,
10 was jemand geheim mir aufgetragen.

Eva

Wer denn? Der Junker?

Magdalene

　　　　　Nichts da! Nein!
Beckmesser.

Eva

　　　Das mag 'was Rechtes sein!
(They go into the house.)

Sachs, in light indoor dress, returns to the workshop. He turns
to *David*, who is still at work.

Sachs

Zeig' her! — 's ist gut. — Dort an die Tür'
rück' mir Tisch und Schemel herfür! —
5 Leg' dich zu Bett! Wach' auf bei Zeit,
verschlaf' die Dummheit, sei morgen gescheit!

2. **heraus**: see Vocab. 3. **sprach** = *sah*. 12. **Rechtes**: see *recht*.

David (arranges bench and stool).

Schafft ihr noch Arbeit?

Sachs

Kümmert dich das?

David (aside).

Was war nur der Lene? — Gott weiss, was! —
Warum wohl der Meister heute wacht?

Sachs

Was steh'st noch?

David

Schlaft wohl, Meister!

Sachs

Gut' Nacht!

(*David* goes into the chamber.)

Sachs

(arranges his work, seats himself on the stool at the door, then laying
aside his work again leans back, and rests his arm on the lower half
of the shop door).

5   Wie duftet doch der Flieder
so mild, so stark und voll!
Mir lös't es weich die Glieder,
will, dass ich was sagen soll. —
Was gilt's, was ich dir sagen kann?
10   Bin gar ein arm einfältig Mann!
Soll mir die Arbeit nicht schmecken,
gäb'st, Freund, lieber mich frei:
tät' besser das Leder zu strecken,
und liess alle Poeterei. —

(Takes up his work again, lays it aside and reflects).

15   Und doch, 's will halt nicht geh'n. —
Ich fühl's — und kann's nicht versteh'n —
kann's nicht behalten, — doch auch nicht vergessen;
und fass' ich es ganz, — kann ich's nicht messen! —
Doch wie auch wollt' ich's fassen,
20   was unermesslich mir schien?
Kein' Regel wollte da passen,
und war doch kein Fehler drin. —

2. **Was war**...=*was fehlte.* 11. **Soll** = *wenn,* clause. 12. **Freund**
= *der Flieder.*

Es klang so alt, und war doch so neu, —·
wie Vogelsang im süssen Mai : —
      wer ihn hört,
      und wahnbetört
5   sänge dem Vogel nach,
     dem brächt' es Spott und Schmach. —
      Lenzes Gebot,
      die süsse Not,
     die legten's ihm in die Brust :
10   nun sang er, wie er musst' !
     Und wie er musst', so konnt' er's :
     das merkt' ich ganz besonders :
     dem Vogel, der heut' sang,
dem war der Schnabel hold gewachsen ;
15   macht' er den Meistern bang,
gar wohl gefiel er doch Hans Sachsen.

Eva appears on the street and shyly approaches the workshop.

Eva

Gut'n Abend, Meister !   Noch so fleissig ?
      Sachs (starting up with pleased surprise).
Ei, Kind !   Lieb' Evchen ?   Noch so spät ?
Und doch, warum so spät noch, weiss ich :
20 die neuen Schuh' ?

Eva

      Wie fehl er rät !
Die Schuh' hab' ich noch gar nicht probiert
die sind so schön, so reich geziert,
dass ich sie noch nicht an die Füss' mir getraut.

Sachs

Doch sollst sie morgen tragen als Braut ?

8. **Not**: Walther *must* sing to win Eva.   20. From this point to the
end of the interview, p. 68, l. 8, Eva's words are full of naive roguish-
ness, also often ambiguous.   She has in reality come to talk with her
good friend Sachs concerning the fate of her lover in his trial before
the masters.   Sachs, however, answers her evasively and ironically.
With tender flattery she suggests that her friend himself enter the contest for her hand, well knowing that he long ago has comprehended
her, and her love for Walther.   But Sachs will not understand her and
in order to entrap her into a confession of love for Walther, pretends
to side with the Masters against Walther.

Eva (seats herself near *Sachs* on the stone bench).
Wer wäre denn Bräutigam?

Sachs
Weiss ich das?

Eva
Wie wisst denn ihr, dass ich Braut?

Sachs
Ei was!
Das weiss die Stadt.

Eva
Ja, weiss es die Stadt,
Freund Sachs gute Gewähr dann hat.
5 Ich dacht', er wüsst' mehr.

Sachs
Was sollt' ich wissen?

Eva
Ei seht doch! Werd' ich's ihm sagen müssen?
Ich bin wohl recht dumm?

Sachs
Das sag' ich nicht.

Eva.
Dann wär't ihr wohl klug?

Sachs
Das weiss ich nicht.

Eva
Ihr wisst nichts? Ihr sagt nichts? — Ei, Freund Sachs,
10 jetzt merk' ich wahrlich, Pech ist kein Wachs.
Ich hätt' euch für feiner gehalten.

Sachs
Kind!
Beid', Wachs und Pech vertraut mir sind.
Mit Wachs strich ich die Seidenfäden,
damit ich die zieren Schuh' dir gefasst:
15 heut' fass' ich die Schuh mit dicht'ren Drähten,
da gilt's mit Pech für den derben Gast.

Eva
Wer ist denn der? Wohl 'was Rechts?

Sachs
Das mein' ich!
Ein Meister stolz auf Freiers Fuss,
denkt morgen zu siegen ganz alleinig:
Herrn Beckmessers Schuh ich richten muss.

Eva
So nehmt nur tüchtig Pech dazu:
5 da kleb' er drin, und lass' mir Ruh'!

Sachs
Er hofft dich sicher zu ersingen.

Eva
Wie so denn der?

Sachs
Ein Junggesell:
's gibt deren wenig dort zur Stell'.

Eva
Könnt's einem Witwer nicht gelingen?

Sachs
10 Mein Kind, der wär' zu alt für dich.

Eva
Ei was, zu alt! Hier gilt's der Kunst:
wer sie versteht, der werb' um mich!

Sachs
Lieb' Evchen! Machst mir blauen Dunst?

Eva
Nicht ich! Ihr seid's; ihr macht mir Flausen!
15 Gesteht nur, dass ihr wandelbar;
Gott weiss, wer jetzt euch im Herzen mag hausen
Glaubt' ich mich doch drin so manches Jahr.

Sachs
Wohl, da ich dich gern in den Armen trug?

Eva
Ich seh', 's war nur, weil ihr kinderlos.

Sachs
20 Hatt' einst ein Weib und **Kinder** genug.

Eva

Doch starb eure Frau, so wuchs ich gross.

Sachs

Gar gross und schön!

Eva

Drum dacht' ich aus:
ihr nähm't mich für Weib und Kind ins Haus.

Sachs

Da hätt' ich ein Kind und auch ein Weib:
5 's wär' gar ein lieber Zeitvertreib!
Ja, ja! das hast du dir schön erdacht.

Eva

Ich glaub', der Meister mich gar verlacht?
Am End' gar liess' er sich auch gefallen,
dass unter der Nas' ihm weg von allen
10 der Beckmesser morgen mich ersäng'?

Sachs

Wie sollt' ich's wehren, wenn's ihm geläng'?
Dem wüsst' allein dein Vater Rat.

Eva

Wo so ein Meister den Kopf nur hat!
Käm' ich zu euch wohl, fänd' ich's zu Haus?

Sachs

15 Ach, ja! Hast Recht! 's ist im Kopf mir kraus:
hab' heut' manch' Sorg' und Wirr' erlebt:
da mag's dann sein, dass 'was drin klebt.

Eva

Wohl in der Singschul'? 's war heut' Gebot.

Sachs

Ja, Kind: eine Freiung machte mir Not.

Eva

20 Ja, Sachs! Das hättet ihr gleich soll'n sagen;
plagt' euch dann nicht mit unnützen Fragen. —
Nun sagt, wer war's, der Freiung begehrt?

Sachs

Ein Junker, Kind, gar unbelehrt.

Eva

Ein Junker? Mein, sagt! — und ward er gefreit?

Sachs

Nichts da, mein Kind! 's gab gar viel Streit.

Eva

So sagt! Erzählt, wie ging es zu?
Macht's euch Sorg', wie liess' mir es Ruh'? —
5 So bestand er übel und hat vertan?

Sachs

Ohne Gnad' versang der Herr Rittersmann.

Magdalene (approaches and calls softly).

Bst! Evchen! Bst!

Eva

Ohne Gnade? Wie?
Kein Mittel gäb's, das ihm gedieh'?
Sang er so schlecht, so fehlervoll,
10 dass nichts mehr zum Meister ihm helfen soll?

Sachs

Mein Kind, für den ist alles verloren,
und Meister wird der in keinem Land;
denn wer als Meister ward geboren,
der hat unter Meistern den schlimmsten Stand.

Magdalene (coming nearer).

15 Der Vater verlangt.

Eva

So sagt mir noch an,
ob keinen der Meister zum Freund er gewann?

Sachs

Das wär' nicht übel! Freund ihm noch sein!
Ihm, vor dem all' sich fühlten so klein!
Den Junker Hochmut, lasst ihn laufen,
20 mag er durch die Welt sich raufen:
was wir erlernt mit Not und Müh',
dabei lasst uns in Ruh' verschnaufen!
Hier renn' er nichts uns über'n Haufen,
sein Glück ihm anderswo erblüh'!

23. **Haufen:** see *Haufe.* 24. **erblüh'** = subjunctive.

Eva (rising suddenly).

Ja, anderswo soll's ihm erblüh'n,
als bei euch garst'gen, neid'schen Mannsen;
wo warm die Herzen noch erglüh'n,
trotz allen tück'schen Meister Hansen! —
5 Ja, Lene! Gleich! ich komme schon!
Was trüg' ich hier für Trost davon?
Da riecht's nach Pech, dass Gott erbarm'!
Brennt' er's lieber, da würd' er doch warm!

She crosses over hastily with *Magdalene* and pauses, much excited,
at her own door.

Sachs (with a significant nod).

Das dacht' ich wohl.   Nun heisst's: schaff' Rat!

During the following, he closes the upper half of the shop door,
so as to leave only a little ray of light shining through a crack; he
himself is quite invisible.

Magdalene

10 Hilf Gott! was bliebst du nur so spat?
Der Vater rief.

Eva

Geh' zu ihm ein:
ich sei zu Bett im Kämmerlein.

Magdalene

Nicht doch! Hör' nur! Komm ich dazu?
Beckmesser fand mich: er lässt nicht Ruh',
15 zur Nacht sollst du dich ans Fenster neigen,
er will dir 'was Schönes singen und geigen,
mit dem er dich hofft zu gewinnen, das Lied,
ob dir das zu Gefallen geriet.

Eva

Das fehlte auch noch! — Käme nur Er!

Magdalene

20 Hast' David geseh'n?

Eva

Was soll mir der?

Magdalene (half aside).

Ich war zu streng; er wird sich grämen.

4. **Meister Hansen** = Hans Sachs.   12. Understand "and say"
before the line.

Eva

Siehst du noch nichts?

Magdalene

's ist als ob Leut' dort kämen.

Eva

Wär' er's?

Magdalene

Mach' und komm jetzt hinan!

Eva

Nicht eh'r, bis ich sah den teuersten Mann!

Magdalene

Ich täuschte mich dort: er war es nicht. —
5 Jetzt komm, sonst merkt der Vater die G'schicht'!

Eva

Ach! meine Angst!

Magdalene

Auch lass uns beraten,
wie wir des Beckmessers uns entladen.

Eva

Zum Fenster gehst du für mich.

Magdalene

Wie, ich? —
Das machte wohl David eiferlich?
10 Er schläft nach der Gassen! Hihi! 's wär' fein! —

Eva

Dort hör' ich Schritte.

Magdalene

Jetzt komm', es muss sein!

Eva

Jetzt näher!

Magdalene

Du irrst! 's ist nichts, ich wett'.
Ei, komm! Du musst, bis der Vater zu Bett.

(*Pogner's* voice from within.)

He! Lene! Eva!

2. **hinan:** see *hinan.*

Magdalene

's ist höchste Zeit!
Hörst du's? Komm'! der Ritter ist weit.

Walther comes up the alley, and now turns the corner by *Pogner's* house. *Eva*, who has been dragged along by *Magdalene*, tears herself away, and with a soft cry rushes toward *Walther*.

Eva

Da ist er!

Magdalene (going in).

Nun haben wir's! Jetzt heisst's: gescheit!
(Exit.)

Eva (beside herself).

Ja, ihr seid es!
Nein, du bist es!
5   alles sag' ich,
denn ihr wisst es,
alles klag' ich,
denn ich weiss es;
ihr seid beides,
10   Held des Preises,
und mein einz'ger Freund!

Walther (passionately).

Ach, du irrst! Bin nur dein Freund,
doch des Preises
noch nicht würdig,
15   nicht den Meistern
ebenbürtig:
mein Begeistern
fand Verachten,
und ich weiss es,
20   darf nicht trachten
nach der Freundin Hand!

Eva

Wie du irrst! Der Freundin Hand,
erteilt nur sie den Preis,
wie deinen Mut ihr Herz erfand,
25   reicht sie nur dir das Reis.

Walther

Ach nein! du irrst! Der Freundin Hand,
wär' keinem sie erkoren,

wie sie des Vaters Wille band,
mir wär' sie doch verloren.
"Ein Meistersinger muss er sein:
Nur wen ihr krönt, den darf sie frei'n!"
5 So sprach er festlich zu den Herrn,
kann nicht zurück, möcht' er's auch gern!
Das eben gab mir Mut;
wie ungewohnt mir alles schien,
ich sang mit Lieb' und Glut,
10 dass ich den Meisterschlag verdien'.
Doch diese Meister!
Ha, diese Meister!
Dieser Reim-Gesetze
Leimen und Kleister!
15 Mir schwillt die Galle,
das Herz mir stockt,
denk' ich der Falle,
darein ich gelockt! —
Fort, in die Freiheit!
20 Dorthin gehör' ich,
da wo ich Meister im Haus!
Soll ich dich frei'n heut',
dich nun beschwör' ich,
flieh', und folg' mir hinaus!
25 Keine Wahl ist offen,
nichts steht zu hoffen!
Überall Meister,
wie böse Geister,
seh' ich sich rotten
30 mich zu verspotten:
mit den Gewerken,
aus den Gemerken,
aus allen Ecken,
auf allen Flecken,
35 seh' ich zu Haufen
Meister nur laufen,
mit höhnendem Nicken
frech auf dich blicken,
in Kreisen und Ringeln
40 dich umzingeln,
näselnd und kreischend

zur Braut dich heischend.
als Meisterbuhle
auf dem Singestuhle,
zitternd und bebend,
5   hoch dich erhebend : —
und ich ertrüg' es, sollt' es nicht wagen,
grad' aus tüchtig drein zu schlagen ?

The loud sound of the nightwatchman's horn is heard. *Walther*
lays his hand on his sword with a quick gesture and stares wildly
before him.

Ha ! . . .

Eva (grasps his hand soothingly).

Geliebter, spare den Zorn !
10   's war nur des Nachtwächters Horn. —
Unter der Linde
birg' dich geschwinde :
hier kommt der Wächter vorbei.

Magdalene (at the door, softly).

Evchen ! 's ist Zeit : mach' dich frei !

Walther

15   Du fliehst ?

Eva

Muss ich denn nicht ?

Walther

Entweichst ?

Eva

Dem Meistergericht.

(She disappears into the house with *Magdalene.*)

Der Nachtwächter

(has meanwhile appeared in the alley, comes forward singing, turns
the corner at *Pogner's* house, goes further and disappears to the left).

"Hört ihr Leut', und lasst euch sagen,
die Glock' hat Zehn geschlagen :
bewahrt das Feuer und auch das Licht,
20   damit niemand kein Schad' geschicht !
Lobet Gott den Herrn !"

(After he has disappeared, his horn is still heard.)

20. **geschicht** = *geschieht,*

Sachs

(who has been listening at the shop door, now opens it a little wider,
having shaded his lamp).

Üble Dinge, die ich da merk':
eine Entführung gar im Werk!
Aufgepasst! das darf nicht sein!

Walther (behind the linden).

Käm' sie nicht wieder?   O der Pein! —
5 Doch ja! sie kommt dort! — Weh' mir, nein!
Die Alte ist's! — doch aber — ja!

Eva

(returns in *Magdalene's* clothes and goes to *Walther*).

Das tör'ge Kind: da hast du's da!

(She sinks on his breast.)

Walther.

O Himmel! Ja! nun wohl ich weiss,
dass ich gewann den Meisterpreis.

Eva.

10 Doch nun kein Besinnen!
Von hinnen! Von hinnen!
O wären wir weit schon fort!

Walther.

Hier durch die Gasse: dort
finden wir vor dem Tor
15 Knecht und Rosse vor.

As they both turn to go into the alley, *Sachs*, after putting the
lamp behind a globe, lets a bright stream of light through the now
wide open door on to the street, so that *Walther* and *Eva* find themselves plainly visible.

Eva (hastily pulling *Walther* back).

O weh', der Schuster! Wenn er uns säh'!
Bırg' dich! komm ihm nicht in die Näh'!

Walther

Welch andrer Weg führt uns hinaus?

Eva (pointing to the right).

Dort durch die Strasse: doch der ıst kraus,
20 ich kenn' ihn nicht gut; auch stiessen wir dort
auf den Wächter.

4. **der Pein:** genitive absolute.

Walther

Nun denn : durch die Gasse !

Eva

Der Schuster muss erst vom Fenster fort.

Walther

Ich zwing' ihn, dass er's verlasse.

Eva.

Zeig' dich ihm nicht : er kennt dich !

Walther

Der Schuster ?

Eva

's ist Sachs !

Walther

Hans Sachs ? Mein Freund ?

Eva

Glaub's nicht !

5 Von dir zu sagen Übles nur wusst' er.

Walther

Wie, Sachs ? Auch er ? Ich lösch' ihm das Licht !

Beckmesser comes up the alley creeping along at some distance after the *Watchman*. He watches cautiously the windows of *Pogner's* house, and, leaning against *Sachs's* house, seeks out a stone seat between the two windows, on which he seats himself, all the while watching the windows opposite, and now begins to tune a lute he has with him.

Eva (restraining *Walther*).

Tu's nicht ! — Doch horch !

Walther

Einer Laute Klang ?

Eva

Ach, meine Not !

Walther

Wie, wird dir bang ?

Der Schuster, sieh, zog ein das Licht : —

10 so sei's gewagt !

Eva

Weh' ! Hörst du denn nicht ?

Ein andrer kam, und nahm dort Stand.

Walther

Ich hör's und seh's : — ein Musikant.
Was will der hier so spät des Nachts ?

Eva

's ist Beckmesser schon !

Sachs

(on hearing the first tones of the lute, sets the lamp back a little,
and then, as if an idea occurred to him, softly opens the lower half of
the work-shop door and places his work-bench in the entrance.   He
now hears *Eva's* words).

Aha ! ich dacht's !

Walther

Der Merker !   Er ? in meiner Gewalt ?
5 Drauf zu ! den Lung'rer mach' ich kalt !

Eva

Um Gott !   So hör' !   Willst den Vater wecken ?
Er singt ein Lied, dann zieht er ab.
Lass dort uns im Gebüsch verstecken. —
Was mit den Männern ich Müh' doch hab' !

(She draws *Walther* to the bench behind the bushes which surround
the linden.)

Beckmesser

(full of impatience, tinkles on his lute to see if the window will not
be opened.   Just as he is on the point of singing, *Sachs*, who has let
the light fall full upon the street, begins to hammer upon his last and
sing with immense vigor).

Sachs

10   Jerum !   Jerum !
           Halla halla he !
        Oho !   Trallalei ! O he !
     Als Eva aus dem Paradies
           von Gott dem Herrn verstossen,
15   gar schuf ihr Schmerz der harte Kies
           an ihrem Fuss dem blossen.
         Das jammerte den Herrn,
           ihr Füsschen hat er gern,
     und seinem Engel rief er zu :
20   "da mach' der armen Sünd'rin Schuh' !

2. **des Nachts:** by analogy from *des Tages.* 10–11. *Jauchzer-
bildungen,* translatable by words of similar type in English.

Und da der Adam, wie ich seh',
an Steinen dort sich stösst die Zeh',
dass recht fortan
er wandeln kann,
so miss' dem auch Stiefeln an !"

Walther (to *Eva*).

Wie heisst das Lied?   Wie nennt er dich?

Eva

Ich hört' es schon : 's geht nicht auf mich.
Doch eine Bosheit steckt darin.

Walther

Welch Zögernis !   Die Zeit geht hin !

Beckmesser (as *Sachs* begins to sing).

Was soll das sein? —
Verdammtes Schrein !
Was fällt dem groben Schuster ein?

(Stepping forward).

Wie, Meister ?   Auf?   So spät zur Nacht?

Sachs

Herr Stadtschreiber !   Was, ihr wacht? —
Die Schuh' machen euch grosse Sorgen?
Ihr seht, ich bin dran : ihr habt sie morgen.

Beckmesser

Hol' der Teufel die Schuh' !
Ich will hier Ruh' !

Sachs (while at work).

Jerum !   Jerum !
Halla halla he !
O ho !   Trallalei !   O he !
O Eva !   Eva !   Schlimmes Weib !
Das hast du am Gewissen,
dass ob der Füss' am Menschenleib
jetzt Engel schustern müssen.
Bliebst du im Paradies,
Da gab es keinen Kies.
Ob deiner jungen Missetat
handtier' ich jetzt mit Ahl' und Draht,

---

11. Schrein = *Schreien*.

und ob Herrn Adam's übler Schwäch'
versohl' ich Schuh' und streiche Pech.
    Wär' ich nicht fein
    ein Engel rein,
5   Teufel möchte Schuster sein !

Beckmesser	**Walther**
	(to *Eva*)
Gleich höret auf !	
Spielt ihr Streich' ?	Uns, oder dem Merker ?
Bleibt ihr Tag's	Wem spielt er den Streich ?
und Nachts euch gleich !	
Sachs	**Eva**
	(to *Walther*)
10 Wenn ich hier sing',	Ich fürcht', uns dreien
was kümmert's euch ?	gilt es gleich.
Die Schuhe sollen	O weh, der Pein !
doch fertig werden ?	Mir ahnt nichts Gutes !
Beckmesser	**Walther**
So schliesst euch ein	Mein süsser Engel,
15 und schweigt dazu still !	sei guten Mutes !
Sachs	**Eva**
Des Nachts arbeiten	Mich betrübt das Lied !
macht Beschwerden ;	**Walther**
Wenn ich da munter	
bleiben will,	Ich hör' es kaum !
20 da brauch' ich Luft	Du bist bei mir :
und frischen Gesang ;	Welch holder Traum !
drum hört wie der dritte	(Embraces *Eva* tenderly.)
Vers gelang !	

    Beckmesser (while *Sachs* is singing).
Er macht mich rasend ! — Das grobe Geschrei !
25 Am End' denkt sie gar, das ich das sei !

    Sachs (still at work).
    Jerum ! Jerum !
    Halla halla he !
    O ho ! Trallalei ! O he !
    O Eva ! Hör' mein Klageruf,
30   mein Not und schwer Verdrüssen !

10. **dreien**: declined form of *drei*. 12. **der Pein**: see note p. 73,
l. 4. 15. **guten Mutes**: genitive absolute.

Die Kunstwerk', die ein Schuster schuf,
    sie tritt die Welt mit Füssen!
Gäb' nicht ein Engel Trost,
    der gleiches Werk erlos't,
5   und rief mich oft ins Paradies,
wie dann ich Schuh' und Stiefel liess'!
Doch wenn der mich im Himmel hält,
dann liegt zu Füssen mir die Welt,
      und bin in Ruh'
10   Hans Sachs ein Schuh-
    macher und Poet dazu.

Beckmesser (watching the window, which now softly opens).

Das Fenster geht auf: — Herr Gott, 's ist sie!

Eva (to *Walther*).

Mich schmerzt das Lied, ich weiss nicht wie!
O fort, lass' uns fliehen!

Walther (half drawing his sword).

          Nun denn: mit dem Schwert!

Eva

15 Nicht doch!   Ach halt'!

Walther

          Kaum wär' er's wert!

Eva

Ja, besser Geduld!   O lieber Mann!
Dass ich so Not dir machen kann!

Walther

Wer ist am Fenster?

Eva

      's ist Magdalene.

Walther

Dass heiss' ich vergelten! fast muss ich lachen.

Eva

20 Wie ich ein End' und Flucht mir ersehne!

Walther

Ich wünscht' er möchte den Anfang machen.

(They follow proceedings with increasing interest.)

4. **Der**: relative pronoun to *Engel* and subject to *erlos't.* — erlos't
= *erlös't.*

Beckmesser (who, while *Sachs* continues to sing, has taken counsel with himself in great excitement).

Jetzt bin ich verloren, singt der noch fort! —
(He walks to the shop.)

Freund Sachs! So hört doch nur ein Wort!
Wie seid ihr auf die Schuh' versessen!
Ich hatt' sie wahrlich schon vergessen.
5 Als Schuster seid ihr mir wohl wert,
als Kunstfreund doch weit mehr verehrt.
Eu'r Urteil glaubt, das halt' ich hoch;
drum bitt' ich: hört das Liedlein doch,
mit dem ich morgen möcht' gewinnen,
10 ob das auch recht nach euren Sinnen.

(Keeping his back turned to the alley, he tinkles on the lute to hold the attention of *Magdalene* and keep her at the window.)

Sachs

O ha! Wollt mich beim Wahne fassen?
Mag mich nicht wieder schelten lassen.
Seit sich der Schuster dünkt Poet,
gar übel es um eu'r Schuhwerk steht;
15   ich seh' wie's schlappt,
    und überall klappt:
    drum lass' ich Vers' und Reim'
    gar billig nun daheim,
    Verstand und Kenntnis auch dazu,
20 mach' euch für morgen die neuen Schuh'.

Beckmesser (tinkling on his lute as before).

Lasst das doch sein! das war ja nur Scherz.
Vernehmt besser, wie's mir ums Herz!
    Vom Volk seid ihr geehrt,
    auch der Pognerin seid ihr wert:
25 will ich vor aller Welt
nun morgen um die werben,
sagt, könnt's mich nicht verderben,
wenn mein Lied euch nicht gefällt?
Drum hört mich ruhig an;
30   und sang ich, sagt mir dann,
    was euch gefällt, was nicht,
    dass ich mich danach richt'. (Tinkles again.)

13–20. Sachs good naturedly retaliates on Beckmesser by making use of the latter's words. Cf. p. 52, lines 11—18. 24. **Pognerin**=*Eva*.

Sachs

Ei lasst mich doch in Ruh'!
Wie käm' solche Ehr' mir zu?
Nur Gassenhauer dicht' ich zum meisten:
drum sing' ich zur Gassen, und hau' auf den Leisten.

(Working again.)

5   Jerum! Jerum!
Halla halla hei!

Beckmesser

Verfluchter Kerl! — Den Verstand verlier' ich,
mit seinem Lied von Pech und Schmierich! —
Schweigt doch!   Weckt ihr die Nachbarn auf?

Sachs

10 Die sind's gewohnt: 's hört keiner drauf. —
"O Eva! Eva! schlimmes Weib!" —

Beckmesser (in a rage).

O ihr boshafter Geselle!
Ihr spielt mir heut' den letzten Streich!
Schweigt ihr nicht auf der Stelle,
15   so denkt ihr dran, das schwör' ich euch.
Neidisch seid ihr, nichts weiter,
dünkt ihr euch gleich gescheiter:
dass and're auch 'was sind, ärgert euch schändlich!
Glaubt, ich kenne euch aus- und innwendlich!
20 Dass man euch noch nicht zum Merker gewählt,
das ist's, was den gallichten Schuster quält.
Nun gut! So lang' als Beckmesser lebt,
und ihm noch ein Reim an den Lippen klebt,
so lang' ich noch bei den Meistern 'was gelt',
25   ob Nürnberg "blüh' oder wachs',"
dass schwör' ich Herrn Hans Sachs:
nie wird er je zum Merker bestellt!

(He tinkles again impatiently.)

Sachs (who has listened to him calmly and attentively).
War das eu'r Lied?

Beckmesser

Der Teufel hol's!

13. **'was** = *etwas*. Also in line 24.

Sachs

Zwar wenig Regel : doch klang's recht stolz !

Beckmesser

Wollt ihr mich hören ?

Sachs

In Gottes Namen,
singt zu : ich schlag' auf die Sohl' die Rahmen.

Beckmesser

Doch schweigt ihr still ?

Sachs

Ei, singet ihr,
5 die Arbeit, schaut, fördert's auch mir.

(He continues to hammer on his last.)

Beckmesser

das verfluchte Klopfen wollt ihr doch lassen ?

Sachs

Wie sollt' ich die Sohl' euch richtig fassen ?

Beckmesser

Was ? wollt ihr klopfen, und ich soll singen ?

Sachs

Euch muss das Lied, mir der Schuh gelingen.

(Keeps on knocking.)

Beckmesser

10 Ich mag keine Schuh' !

Sachs

Das sagt ihr jetzt ;
in der Singschul' ihr mir's dann wieder versetzt. —
Doch hört ! Vielleicht sich's richten lässt :
zwei-einig geht der Mensch zu best.
Darf ich die Arbeit nicht entfernen,
15 die Kunst des Merkers möcht' ich doch lernen :
darin nun kommt euch keiner gleich ;
ich lern' sie nie, wenn nicht von euch.
Drum singt ihr nun, ich acht' und merk',
und fördr' auch wohl dabei mein Werk.

Beckmesser

Merkt immer zu ; und was nicht gewann,
nehmt eure Kreide, und streicht's mir an.

Sachs

Nein, Herr, da fleckten die Schuh' mir nicht :
mit dem Hammer auf den Leisten halt' ich Gericht.

Beckmesser

5 Verdammte Bosheit! — Gott, und's wird spät :
am End' mir die Jungfer vom Fenster geht !

(He tinkles as though about to begin.)

Sachs (with a blow on his last.)

Fanget an! 's pressiert !   Sonst sing' ich für mich !

Beckmesser

Haltet ein ! nur das nicht ! — Teufel ! wie ärgerlich ! —
Wollt ihr euch denn als Merker erdreisten,
10 nun gut, so merkt mit dem Hammer auf den Leisten :—
nur mit dem Beding, nach den Regeln scharf ;
aber nichts, was nach den Regeln ich darf.

Sachs

Nach den Regeln, wie sie der Schuster kennt,
dem die Arbeit unter den Händen brennt.

Beckmesser

15 Auf Meister-Ehr' !

Sachs

Und Schuster-Mut !

Beckmesser

Nicht einen Fehler : glatt und gut !

Sachs

Dann gingt ihr morgen unbeschuht. —
Setzt euch denn hier !

Beckmesser (placing himself at the corner of the house).

Lasst hier mich stehen !

Sachs

Warum so fern ?

Beckmesser

Euch nicht zu sehen,
20 wie's Brauch in der Schul' vor dem Gemerk'.

Sachs

Da hör' ich euch schlecht.

Beckmesser

Der Stimme Stärk'
ich so gar lieblich dämpfen kann.

Sachs

Wie fein ! — Nun gut denn ! — Fanget an !

(Short prelude by *Beckmesser* on the lute, whereupon *Magdalene* leans
out of the window.)

Walther (to *Eva*)

Welch' toller Spuck! Mich dünkt's ein Traum :
den Singstuhl, scheint's, verliess ich kaum !

Eva

Die Schläf' umwebt's mir, wie ein Wahn :
ob's Heil, ob Unheil, was ich ahn' ?

(She sinks as though stupefied on *Walther's* breast; they remain thus).

Beckmesser (with his lute).

"Den Tag seh' ich erscheinen,
der mir wohl gefall'n tut . . ."

(*Sachs* knocks. *Beckmesser* starts, but keeps on.)

"Da fasst mein Herz sich einen
guten und frischen Mut."

(*Sachs* knocks twice. *Beckmesser* then turns softly but angrily.)

Treibt ihr hier Scherz ?
Was wär' nicht gelungen ?

8. The false accent of Beckmesser's doggerel is apparent to any
reader.

Any attempt to explain a joke generally ends in explaining it
away. But one is tempted to point out that we are confronted with
the very comical situation of a love-lorn suitor hastening the comple-
tion of his wedding shoes, by the number of mistakes he makes in
serenading his lady-love. Singing well, he loses his shoes, and perhaps, (at least he hopes), wins his lady. Singing poorly, he gets the
shoes by reason of the great number of mistakes, for every mistake is
a peg in the shoe, but loses his lady; and he therefore has little need
for the shoes. Further, remembering the previous relation of "Merker" Beckmesser and "Schuster" Sachs, how Beckmesser has sworn
that Sachs shall never be "Merker," the whole situation is full of
the keenest humor.

Sachs

Besser gesungen:
"da fasst mein Herz
sich einen guten und frischen Mut."

Beckmesser

Wie sollt' sich das reimen
5　　auf "seh' ich erscheinen"?

Sachs

Ist euch an der Weise nichts gelegen?
Mich dünkt, 's sollt' passen Ton und Wort.

Beckmesser

Mit euch hier zu streiten? — Lasst von den Schlägen,
sonst denkt ihr mir dran!

Sachs

　　　　　　　　　Jetzt fahret fort!

Beckmesser

10　Bin ganz verwirrt!

Sachs

　　　　　　So fangt noch 'mal an:
drei Schläg' ich jetzt pausieren kann.

Beckmesser (aside).

Am Besten, wenn ich ihn gar nicht beacht': —
wenn's nur die Jungfer nicht irre macht!

(He clears his throat and begins again.)

"Den Tag seh' ich erscheinen,
15　　der mir wohl gefall'n tut;
da fasst mein Herz sich einen
guten und frischen Mut.
Da denk' ich nicht an Sterben
　　　lieber an Werben
20　　um jung Mägdeleins Hand.
Warum wohl aller Tage
schönster mag dieser sein?
Allen hier ich es sage:
weil ein schönes Fräulein
25　　von ihrem lieb'n Herrn Vater,
wie gelobt hat er,
ist bestimmt zum Eh'stand.

9. **dran** = *daran.* 10. **'mal** = *einmal.*

Wer sich getrau',
der komm' und schau'
da steh'n die hold lieblich Jungfrau,
auf die ich all' mein' Hoffnung bau':
darum ist der Tag so schön blau,
als ich anfänglich fand."

From the sixth line on, *Sachs* has been continually pounding with
his hammer, recording thus the various mistakes. *Beckmesser*, who
quivers at every blow, is compelled, in attempting to control his rage,
to sing in a jerky, ejaculatory fashion. The comical effect of his doggerel performance is thereby much increased. Now he bursts out in a
rage on *Sachs* around the corner.

Beckmesser

Sachs ! — Seht ! — Ihr bringt mich um !
Wollt ihr jetzt schweigen ?

Sachs

Ich bin ja stumm ?
Die Zeichen merkt' ich : wir sprechen dann ;
derweil' lassen die Sohlen sich an.

Beckmesser

(peeping up toward the window and hastily tinkling again).

Sie entweicht ? Bst, Bst ! — Herr Gott ! ich muss
(Shaking his fist at *Sachs* around the corner.)
Sachs !   Euch gedenk' ich die Ärgernuss !

Sachs (raising his hammer over the last).

Merker am Ort ! —
Fahret fort !

Beckmesser

"Will heut' mir das Herz hüpfen,
werben um Fräulein jung,
doch tät der Vater knüpfen
daran ein' Bedingung
für den, wer ihn beerben
will, und auch werben
um sein Kindelein fein.
Der Zunft ein biedrer Meister
wohl sein' Tochter er liebt,

12. **Ärgernuss** = *Ärgernis*.

doch zugleich auch beweist er,
was er auf die Kunst giebt:
zum Preise muss es bringen
im Meistersingen,
5　　wer sein Eidam will sein.
Nun gilt es Kunst,
dass mit Vergunst
ohn' all' schädlich gemeinen Dunst,
ihm glücke des Preises Gewunst,
10　wer begehrt mit wahrer Inbrunst
um die Jungfrau zu frein."

Beckmesser, his eyes fixed on the window, has noticed, with growing fear, *Magdalene's* evident signs of impatience.　In order to drown
out *Sachs's* blows, he begins to sing more loudly and more hurriedly.
He is about to continue, when *Sachs*, knocking out the key of the last
and removing the shoes, rises from the stool and leans out over the
door.

Sachs

Seid ihr nun fertig?

Beckmesser (in extreme anxiety).

Wie fraget ihr?

Sachs (triumphantly holding the shoes out at the door).

Mit den Schuhen ward ich fertig schier! —
Das heiss' ich mir rechte Merkerschuh':
15　mein Merkersprüchlein hört dazu!
mit lang' und kurzen Hieben,
steht's auf der Sohl' geschrieben:
da les't es klar
und nehmt es wahr,
20　und merkt's euch immerdar:
Gut Lied will Takt,
wer den verzwackt,
dem Schreiber mit der Feder
haut ihn der Schuster aufs Leder. —
25　Nun lauft in Ruh',
habt gute Schuh';
der Fuss euch drin nicht knackt;
ihn hält die Sohl' im Takt!

(He laughs loudly.)

9. **Gewunst** = *Gewinnst*.　13. Cf. p. 49, l. 23.

Beckmesser

(who has withdrawn to the alley again, and leaning against *Sachs's* house between the two windows, sings the third verse hastily at the top of his voice in order to drown out *Sachs*).

" Darf ich Meister mich nennen,
das bewähr' ich heut' gern,
weil nach dem Preis ich brennen
muss dursten und hungern.
5 Nun ruf' ich die neun Musen,
  dass an sie blusen
mein dicht'rischen Verstand.
Wohl kenn' ich alle Regeln,
halte gut Mass und Zahl ;
10 doch Sprung und Überkegeln
wohl passiert je einmal,
wann der Kopf, ganz voll Zagen,
  zu frei'n will wagen
um ein' jung Mägdleins Hand.
15 Ein Junggesell,
  trug ich mein Fell,
mein Ehr', Amt, Würd', und Brot zur Stell',
dass euch mein Gesang wohl gefäll',
und mich das Jungfräulein erwähl',
20 wenn sie mein Lied gut fand."

Nachbarn

(first a few, then others open the alley windows and peep out during the song.)

Wer heult denn da ? Wer kreischt mit Macht ?
Ist das erlaubt so spät zur Nacht ? —
Gebt Ruhe hier ! 's ist Schlafenszeit ! —
Nein, hört nur, wie der Esel schreit ! —
25 Ihr da ! Seid still, und schert euch fort !
Heult, kreischt und schreit an and'rem Ort !

David

(likewise opens his window close to *Beckmesser* and peers out).

Wer Teufel hier ? — Und drüben gar ?
Die Lene ist's — ich seh' es klar !
Herrje ! das war's, den hat sie bestellt ;
30 der ist's, der ihr besser als ich gefällt ! —

---

6. **an** . . . **blusen**: vulgar, see *blasen.*

{ Nun warte ! du kriegst's ! dir streich' ich das Fell !
{ Zum Teufel mit dir verdammter Gesell' !

David, armed with a club, springs out of a window, knocks *Beckmesser's* lute out of his hand, and closes with him.

Magdalene

(who, finally, in order to make the Marker go, has made extravagant
gestures of pleasure, now shrieks out loudly):

Ach Himmel ! David ! Gott, welche Not !
Zu Hülfe ! zu Hülfe !   Sie schlagen sich tot !

Beckmesser (fighting with *David*).

5 Verfluchter Kerl !   Lässt du mich los ?

David

Gewiss !   Die Glieder brech' ich dir blos !

(They still struggle and fight.)

Nachbarn (at the windows).

Seht nach ! Springt zu ! Da würgen sich zwei !

Andere Nachbarn (coming into the alley).

Heda ! Herbei ! 's gibt Prügelei !
Ihr da ! auseinander !   Gebt freien Lauf !
10 Lasst ihr nicht los, wir schlagen drauf !

Ein Nachbar

Ei seht ! Auch ihr da ? Geht's euch 'was an ?

Ein Zweiter

Was sucht ihr hier ? Hat man euch 'was gethan ?

Erster Nachbar

Euch kennt man gut !

Zweiter Nachbar

Euch noch viel besser !

Erster Nachbar

Wie so denn ?

Zweiter Nachbar (pitching in).

Ei, so !

Magdalene (screaming down).

David ! Beckmesser !

Lehrbuben (coming up).

15 Herbei ! Herbei ! 's gibt Keilerei !

Einige

's sind die Schuster!

Andere

Nein, 's sind die Schneider!

Die Ersteren

Die Trunkenbolde!

Die Anderen

Die Hungerleider!

Die Nachbarn (in the alley to one another)

Euch gönnt' ich's schon lange! —
Wird euch wohl bange?
5 Das für die Klage! —
Seht euch vor, wenn ich schlage!
⌈ Hat euch die Frau gehetzt? —
 Schau' wie es Prügel setzt! —
 Seid ihr noch nicht gewitzt? —
10 So schlagt doch! — Das sitzt!
 Dass dich, Halunke! —
 Hie Färbertunke! —
 Wartet, ihr Racker!
 Ihr Massabzwacker! —
15 Esel! — Dummrian! —
 Du Grobian! —
 Lümmel du! —
⌊ Drauf und zu!

Lehrbuben (to one another, and to the neighbors).
 Kennt man die Schlosser nicht?
20 Die haben's sicher angericht'! —
 Ich glaub' die Schmiede werden's sein. —
 Die Schreiner seh' ich dort beim Schein. —
 Hei! Schau' die Schäffler dort beim Tanz. —
 Dort seh' die Bader ich im Glanz. —
25 Krämer finden sich zur Hand
 mit Gerstenstang und Zuckerkand;
 mit Pfeffer, Zimmt, Muskatennuss,
  Sie riechen schön,
  Sie riechen schön.
30 doch haben viel Verdruss,
 und bleiben gern vom Schuss. —

Seht nur, der Hase
Hat üb'rall die Nase! —
Meinst du damit etwa mich?
Mein' ich damit etwa dich?
5   Da hast's auf die Schnautze! —
Herr, jetzt setzt's Plautze! —
Hei! Krach! Hagelwetterschlag!
Wo das sitzt, da wächst nichts nach!
Keilt euch wacker,
10   hau't die Racker!
Haltet selbst Gesellen Stand;
wer da wich', 's wär' wahrlich Schand'!
Drauf und dran!
Wie ein Mann
15   steh'n wir alle zur Keilerei!

(Gradually the *Neighbors* and the *Apprentices* get into a
general fight.)

Gesellen (arriving from all quarters).

Heda! Gesellen 'ran!
Dort wird mit Streit und Zank getan.
Da gibt's gewiss gleich Schlägerei;
Gesellen, haltet euch dabei!
20   'Sind die Weber und Gerber! —
Dacht' ich's doch gleich! —
Die Preisverderber!
Spielen immer Streich'! —
Dort den Metzger Klaus
25   den kennt man heraus!
Zünfte! Zünfte!
Zünfte heraus!
Schneider mit dem Bügel!
Hei! hie setzt's Prügel!
30   Gürtler! — Zinngiesser! —
Leimsieder! — Lichtgiesser! —
Tuchscherer her!
Leinweber her!
Hieher! Hieher!
35   Immer mehr! Immer mehr!

6. **Plautze** = Platze.   7. **Hagelwetterschlag**: 'fire and fury.' or
some such expression.   16. **'ran** = *heran*.   24. **Klaus**: proper name.
34. **hieher** = *hierher*.

Nur tüchtig drauf! Wir schlagen los:
jetzt wird die Keilerei erst gross! —
Lauft heim, sonst kriegt ihr's von der Frau;
hier gibt's nur Prügel-Färbeblau!
  Immer 'ran!
  Mann für Mann!
  Schlagt sie nieder!
Zünfte! Zünfte! Heraus! —

  Die Meister (and old citizens arriving on all sides).

Was gibt's denn da für Zank und Streit?
Das tos't ja weit und breit!
Gebt Ruh' und scher' sich jeder heim,
sonst schlag' ein Hageldonnerwetter drein!
Stemmt euch hier nicht mehr zu Hauf,
oder sonst wir schlagen drauf. —

  Die Nachbarinnen (at the window, to one another).

Was ist denn da für Streit und Zank?
's wird einem wahrlich Angst und bang!
Da ist mein Mann gewiss dabei:
gewiss kommt's noch zur Schlägerei!
  He da! Ihr dort unten,
  so seid doch nur gescheit!
  Seid ihr zu Streit und Raufen
  gleich alle so bereit?
Was für ein Zanken und Toben!
Da werden schon Arme erhoben!
Hört doch! Hört doch!
Seid ihr denn toll?
Sind euch die Köpfe
vom Weine noch voll?
Zu Hülfe! Zu Hülfe!
Da schlägt sich mein Mann!
Der Vater! der Vater!
Sieht man das an?
Christian! Peter!
Niklaus! Hans!
Auf! schreit Zeter! —
Hörst du nicht, Franz?
Gott! wie sie walken!
's wackeln die Zöpfe!

Wasser her! Wasser her!
Giesst's ihn auf die Köpfe!

(The tumult becomes general. Shrieks and blows.)

Magdalene (at the window wrings her hands despairingly).

Ach Himmel! Meine Not ist gross! —
David! So hör' mich doch nur an!
So lass' doch nur den Herren los!

Pogner

(in his nightgown steps to the window and pulls *Magdalene* in).

Um Gott! Eva! schliess' zu! —
Ich seh', ob im Haus unten Ruh'!

The window is closed, and immediately after *Pogner* appears at the house door.

Sachs, at the beginning of the row, has put out the light, and through a crack in the door watches the place under the linden.

Walther and *Eva* have watched the growing tumult with increasing anxiety. *Walther* now takes *Eva* in his arms.

Walther

Jetzt gilt's zu wagen,
sich durchzuschlagen!

Swinging his sword, he presses into the center of the stage. With a bound, *Sachs* rushes out of the shop and seizes *Walther* by the arm.

Pogner (on the steps).

He! Lene! Wo bist du?

Sachs (pushing the half fainting Eva up the steps).

Ins Haus, Jungfer Lene!

(*Pogner* receives her and draws her in by the arm.)

Sachs, flourishing his knee-strap, with which he has already cleared his way to *Walther*, now gives *David* a blow and kicking him into the shop, drags *Walther*, whom he holds with the other hand, into the house with him, and locks the door behind them.

Beckmesser, freed from *David* by *Sachs*, seeks to flee hastily through the crowd.

As soon as *Sachs* has rushed into the street, the *Nightwatchman's* horn is heard sounding loudly at right and front.

Apprentices, *Citizens* and *Journeymen*, all take hasty flight in every direction, so that the stage is speedily and completely cleared. All doors are closed and the women disappear from the windows, which are shut. The full moon appears, and shines brightly into the alley.

Der Nachtwächter

(enters front of stage on the right, rubs his eyes, looks confusedly about, shakes his head, and in a somewhat trembling voice, gives his cry):

Hört ihr Leut', und lasst euch sagen :
die Glock' hat Eilfe geschlagen,
Bewahrt euch vor Gespenstern und Spuck,
dass kein böser Geist eur' Seel' beruck' !
5   Lobet Gott den Herrn !

While singing, he goes slowly up the alley.   As the curtain falls, the sound of his horn is heard several times.

[This second act is perhaps the most beautiful, at any rate the most characteristic and most persuasive portion of the entire work. In Sachs's monologue, in the dialogue under the elders between Sachs and Eva, in the love-scene between Walther and Eva, we find the sweetest strains, melodies of a depth and tenderness not excelled in any other of the master's works.   And then the unique "cobblers' song," Beckmesser's comic serenade, the grotesque and ridiculous street row, all these pass before our vision like a fanciful spectral drama, which the mysterious magic of Johannisnacht has invoked.]

1. The proverbial policeman appears after all is over.   2. **Eilfe** = *Elfe.* 3. **Spuck** = *Spuk* 4. **beruck'** = *berücken.*

DRITTER AUFZUG*

In *Sachs's* workshop. (Front scene.) At the back the half open shop door leading to the street.. At the right, the door of a chamber. At the left, a window opening into the alley, flower-pots before it, a work-bench beside it. *Sachs* is sitting in a large armchair at this window, through which the morning sun is streaming upon him. He has a large folio in his lap, and is absorbed in reading. — *David* peers in at the door from the street. When he sees that *Sachs* takes no notice of him, he steps in with a basket on his arm, which he first hides stealthily under the work-bench, then, feeling reassured that *Sachs* has not noticed him, he cautiously takes it out again, and investigates its contents. He brings to view flowers, ribbon, and at last finds at the bottom a sausage and a cake. He is about to devour these, when *Sachs*, who has not noticed him at all, turns over a leaf of the book with a loud rustle.

David (starts up, conceals the food and turns round).

Gleich! Meister! Hier! —
Die Schuh' sind abgegeben
in Herrn Beckmessers Quartier. —
Mir war's, ihr rief't mich eben?

* After the noise and uproar of the evening, the city has relapsed into its normal peaceful slumbers. Morning approaches, and joyously the sun greets Johannistag. Its clear rays dispel the ghostly forms of the night. Peace and joyous anticipation are throned in every heart. We find Hans Sachs, clad in festive garments, seated in his workroom, meditating on the great world and its seething humanity. Hans Sachs, the "Cobbler Poet," the kind, wise friend, is now presented to us as Hans Sachs, the philosopher. The "need" of the world, the vanity and madness of humanity now form the subject of his contemplation. The accompanying music reminds us of the forest scene in *Siegfried*, where the midday sun illumines the trembling foliage, beneath which Siegfried rests; or of the Good Friday music in *Parsifal* when the morning dew lies on the glittering meadows. With all the wealth and power of his genius, the master paints in the truest, tenderest colors the romance and charm of the mysterious sultry Midsummer's-eve.

The scent of the elders wells in sweet waves; in the stillness the fire-flies take their glittering, capricious course through the darkness. It was in fact this sense-confusing Midsummer's-eve charm which created the disturbance of the night before.

(Aside.)

Er tut, als säh' er mich nicht?
Da ist er bös', wenn er nicht spricht! —

(Approaching very gradually and humbly.)

Ach, Meister! wollt ihr mir verzeih'n!
Kann ein Lehrbub' vollkommen sein?
5 Kenntet ihr die Lene, wie ich,
dann vergäb't ihr mir sicherlich.
Sie ist so gut, so sanft für mich,
und blickt mich oft an, so innerlich:
wenn ihr mich schlagt, streichelt sie mich,
10 und lächelt dabei holdseliglich,
muss ich carieren, füttert sie mich,
und ist in allem gar liebelich.
Nur gestern, weil der Junker versungen,
hab' ich den Korb ihr nicht abgerungen:
15 das schmerzte mich; und da ich fand,
das nachts einer vor dem Fenster stand,
und sang zu ihr, und schrie wie toll,
da hieb ich dem den Buckel voll.
Wie käm' nun da 'was Gross' drauf an?
20 Auch hat's uns'rer Lieb' gar gut getan:
die Lene hat eben mir alles erklärt,
und zum Fest Blumen und Bänder beschert.

(He breaks out in increasing anxiety.)

Ach, Meister! sprecht doch nur ein Wort!

(Aside.)

Hätt' ich nur die Wurst und den Kuchen fort! —

Sachs

(who has read on undisturbed, closes his book. *David* is so frightened by the loud sound that he stumbles and involuntarily falls on his
knees before *Sachs*. The latter, while *David*, still upon his knees,
eyes him with terror, looks over the book in his lap beyond, and his
eyes fall by chance on the table at the back of the stage).

25 Blumen und Bänder seh' ich dort: —
schaut hold und jugendlich aus!
Wie kamen die mir ins Haus?

David (astonished at *Sachs's* friendliness).

Ei, Meister! 's ist heut' hoch festlicher Tag;

10. **holdseliglich** = *holdselig.* 19. **käm . . . an:** see *ankommen.*—
'**was Gross'** = *etwas Grosses.*

da putzt sich jeder, so schön er mag.

Sachs

Wär' Hochzeitsfest?

David

Ja, käm's so weit,
dass David erst die Lene freit!

Sachs

's war Polterabend, dünkt mich doch?

David (aside).

5 Polterabend? — Da krieg' ich's wohl noch? —
(Aloud.)
Verzeiht das, Meister! Ich bitt', vergesst!
Wir feiern ja heut' Johannisfest.

Sachs

Johannisfest?

David (aside).

Hört er heut' schwer?

Sachs

Kannst du dein Sprüchlein? Sag' es her!

David

10 Mein Sprüchlein? Denk', ich kann es gut.
(Aside.)
'Setzt nichts! der Meister ist wohlgemut!
(Aloud.)
"Am Jordan Sankt Johannes stand" —

(In his confusion he has sung his lines to the melody of *Beckmesser's*
serenade in the previous act. *Sachs* makes a gesture of astonishment
and *David* breaks out.)

Verzeiht, Meister; ich kam ins Gewirr:
der Polterabend machte mich irr.

(He continues with the right melody.)

15 "Am Jordan Sankt Johannes stand,
all Volk der Welt zu taufen:
kam auch ein Weib aus fernem Land
von Nürnberg gar gelaufen;
sein Söhnlein trug's zum Uferrand,
20 empfing da Tauf' und Namen;

11. 'Setzt: see *setzen*.

doch als sie dann sich heimgewandt,
      nach Nürnberg wieder kamen,
im deutschen Land gar bald sich fand's
dass wer am Ufer des Jordans
5   Johannes war genannt,
      an der Pegnitz hiess der Hans."
         (Impetuously).
Herr Meister! 's ist heut' eu'r Namenstag!
Nein! Wie man so 'was vergessen mag!
Hier! hier, die Blumen sind für euch,
10 die Bänder, — und was nur alles noch gleich?
Ja hier! schaut, Meister! Herrlicher Kuchen!
Möchtet ihr nicht auch die Wurst versuchen?

      Sachs (still dreamily, without changing position).
Schön Dank, mein Jung'! behalt's für dich!
Doch heut' auf die Wiese begleitest du mich:
15 mit den Bändern und Blumen putz' dich fein;
sollst mein stattlicher Herold sein.

           David
Sollt' ich nicht lieber Brautführer sein? —
Meister! lieb' Meister! ihr müsst wieder frei'n!

           Sachs
Hätt'st wohl gern eine Meist'rin im Haus?

           David
20 Ich mein', es säh' doch viel stattlicher aus.

           Sachs
Wer weiss! Kommt Zeit, kommt Rat.

           David
                              's ist Zeit!
           Sachs
Da wär' der Rat wohl auch nicht weit?

           David
Gewiss geh'n Reden schon hin und wieder.
Den Beckmesser, denk' ich, säng't ihr doch nieder?
25 Ich mein', dass der heut' sich nicht wichtig macht.

           Sachs
Wohl möglich! Hab's mir auch schon bedacht. —

   6. **Pegnitz:** the name of the river running through Nürnberg.

Jetzt geh'; doch stör' mir den Junker nicht!
Komm wieder, wenn du schön gericht'.

David

(kisses *Sachs's* hand with emotion, collects his things and goes into the chamber).

So war er noch nie, wenn sonst auch gut!
Kann mir gar nicht mehr denken, wie der Knieriemen tut!

(Exit.)

Sachs

(still with the book in his lap, leans back absorbed in thought, and after a pause begins):

5 Wahn, Wahn!
Überall Wahn!
Wohin ich forschend blick'
in Stadt- und Welt-Chronik,
den Grund mir aufzufinden,
10 warum gar bis aufs Blut
die Leut sich quälen und schinden
in unnütz toller Wut!
Hat keiner Lohn
noch Dank davon:
15 in Flucht geschlagen
meint er zu jagen.
Hört nicht sein eigen
Schmerz-Gekreisch,
wenn er sich wühlt ins eig'ne Fleisch,
20 wähnt Lust sich zu erzeigen.
Wer gibt den Namen an?
's bleibt halt der alte Wahn,
ohn' den nichts mag geschehen,
's mag gehen oder stehen!
25 steht's wo im Lauf,
er schläft nur neue Kraft sich an;
gleich wacht er auf,
dann schaut wer ihn bemeistern kann! —
Wie friedsam treuer Sitten,
30 getrost in Tat und Werk,
liegt nicht in Deutschlands Mitten

---

2. **gericht'**: see *richten.*   24. **gehen**: see *gehen.*   25. **steht's wo im Lauf**: *wenn* clause.

mein liebes Nürenberg!
Doch eines Abends spat,
ein Unglück zu verhüten
bei jugendheissen Gemüten,
5 ein Mann weiss sich nicht Rat;
ein Schuster in seinem Laden
zieht an des Wahnes Faden:
wie bald auf Gassen und Strassen
fängt der da an zu rasen;
10 Mann, Weib, Gesell und Kind,
fällt sich an wie toll und blind;
und will's der Wahn geseg'nen,
nun muss es Prügel regnen,
mit Hieben, Stoss und Dreschen
15 den Wutesbrand zu löschen. —
Gott weiss, wie das geschah? —
Ein Kobold half wohl da!
Ein Glühwurm fand sein Weibchen nicht;
der hat den Schaden angericht'. —
20 Der Flieder war's: — Johannisnacht. —
Nun aber kam Johannis-Tag: —
jetzt schau'n wir, wie Hans Sachs es macht,
dass er den Wahn fein lenken mag,
ein edler Werk zu tun;
25 denn lässt er uns nicht ruh'n,
selbst hier in Nürenberg,
so sei's um solche Werk',
die selten vor gemeinen Dingen,
und nie ohn' ein'gen Wahn gelingen. —

Walther enters from the chamber door. He pauses there a moment
looking at *Sachs*. The latter turns and lets his book slip to the floor.

Sachs

30 Grüss Gott, mein Junker! Ruhtet ihr noch?
Ihr wachtet lang': nun schlieft ihr doch?

12. **will's ... geseg'nen:** *wenn* clause. 29. Martin Luther's words
are a good commentary on the conclusion of Sachs's monologue. He
says: "God has led me along like a horse that is blindfolded. Good
works are seldom undertaken with knowledge or foresight; everything
that happens is brought about in unconsciousness." Sachs says: "If
we must have the madness even in quiet old Nürnberg, then let us
direct it to the accomplishment of noble ends, such ends as are never
attained without this madness."

Walther (very quietly).

Ein wenig, aber fest und gut.

Sachs

So ist euch nun wohl bass zu Mut?

Walther

Ich hatt' einen wunderschönen Traum.

Sachs

Das deutet Gut's! Erzählt mir den.

Walther

5 Ihn selbst zu denken wag' ich kaum;
ich fürcht' ihn mir vergeh'n zu seh'n.

Sachs

Mein Freund, das grad' ist Dichters Werk,
dass er sein Träumen deut' und merk'.
Glaubt mir, des Menschen wahrster Wahn
10 wird ihm im Traume aufgetan:
all' Dichtkunst und Poeterei
ist nichts als Wahrtraum-Deuterei.
Was gilt's, es gab der Traum euch ein,
wie heut' ihr sollet Sieger sein?

Walther

15 Nein! von der Zunft und ihren Meistern
wollt' sich mein Traumbild nicht begeistern.

Sachs

Doch lehrt' es wohl den Zauberspruch,
mit dem ihr sie gewännet?

Walther

Wie wähnt ihr doch, nach solchem Bruch,
20 wenn ihr noch Hoffnung kennet!

Sachs

Die Hoffnung lass' ich mir nicht mindern,
nichts stiess sie noch über'n Haufen:
wär's nicht, glaubt, statt eure Flucht zu hindern,
wär' ich selbst mit euch fortgelaufen!
25 Drum bitt' ich, lasst den Groll jetzt ruh'n;
ihr habt's mit Ehrenmännern zu tun;

---

2. **bass** = *besser.* 19. **wähnt:** see *wähnen.* 22. **Haufen:** see *Haufen.*

die irren sich, und sind bequem,
dass man auf ihre Weise sie nähm'.
Wer Preise erkennt, und Preise stellt,
der will am End' auch, dass man ihm gefällt.
5 Eu'r Lied das hat ihnen bang' gemacht;
und das mit Recht: denn wohl bedacht,
mit solchem Dicht- und Liebesfeuer
verführt man wohl Töchter zum Abenteuer;
doch für liebseligen Ehestand
10 man andre Wort' und Weisen fand.

Walther (smiling).

Die kenn' ich nun auch, seit dieser Nacht:
es hat viel Lärm auf der Gasse gemacht.

Sachs (laughing).

Ja, ja! Schon gut! Den Takt dazu
den hörtet ihr auch! — Doch, lasst dem Ruh';
15 und folgt meinem Rate, kurz und gut,
fasst zu einem Meisterliede Mut.

Walther

Ein schönes Lied, ein Meisterlied:
wie fass' ich da den Unterschied?

Sachs

Mein Freund! in holder Jugendzeit,
20 wenn uns von mächt'gen Trieben
zum sel'gen ersten Lieben
die Brust sich schwellet hoch und weit,
ein schönes Lied zu singen
mocht' vielen da gelingen:
25 der Lenz, der sang für sie.
Kam Sommer, Herbst und Winterszeit,
viel Not und Sorg' im Leben,
manch' ehlich Glück daneben,
Kindtauf', Geschäfte, Zwist und Streit:
30 denen 's dann noch will gelingen
ein schönes Lied zu singen,
seht, Meister nennt man die. —

Walther.

Ich lieb' ein Weib und will es frei'n,
mein dauernd Ehgemahl zu sein.

Sachs

Die Meisterregeln lernt bei Zeiten,
dass sie getreulich euch geleiten,
    und helfen wohl bewahren,
    was in der Jugend Jahren
5   in holdem Triebe
       Lenz und Liebe
euch unbewusst ins Herz gelegt,
dass ihr das unverloren hegt.

Walther.

Steh'n sie nun in so hohem Ruf,
10 wer ist es, der die Regeln schuf?

Sachs

Das waren hoch-bedürft'ge Meister,
von Lebensmüh' bedrängte Geister;
    in ihrer Nöten Wildnis
    sie schufen sich ein Bildnis,
15   dass ihnen bliebe
      der Jugendliebe
ein Angedenken klar und fest,
dran sich der Lenz erkennen lässt.

Walther

Doch, wem der Lenz schon lang entronnen,
20 wie wird er dem aus dem Bild gewonnen?

Sachs

Er frischt es an, so oft er kann:
drum möcht' ich, als bedürft'ger Mann,
    will ich euch die Regeln lehren,
    sollt ihr sie mir neu erklären. —
25 Seht, hier ist Dinte, Feder, Papier:
ich schreib's euch auf, dictiert ihr mir!

Walther

Wie ich's begänne, wüsst' ich kaum.

Sachs

Erzählt mir euren Morgentraum!

Walther

Durch eurer Regeln gute Lehr',
30 ist mir's, als ob verwischt er wär'.

17. **Angedenken** = *Andenken*.   25. **Dinte** = *Tinte*.

Sachs

Grad' nehmt die Dichtkunst jetzt zur Hand;
mancher durch sie das Verlor'ne fand.

Walther

Dann wär's nicht Traum, doch Dichterei?

Sachs

'Sind Freunde beid', steh'n gern sich bei.

Walther

5 Wie fang' ich nach der Regel an?

Sachs

Ihr stellt sie selbst, und folgt ihr dann.
Gedenkt des schönen Traums am Morgen;
fürs andre lasst Hans Sachs nur sorgen!

1. Gesätz

Walther

(seats himself near *Sachs*, and after some thought begins very softly):

[1. Stolle]

"Morgenlich leuchtend in rosigem Schein,
10   von Blüt' und Duft
     geschwellt die Luft,
     voll aller Wonnen
     nie ersonnen,
   ein Garten lud mich ein
15   Gast ihm zu sein."

(He pauses awhile.)

Sachs

Das war ein Stollen: nun achtet wohl,
dass ganz ein gleicher ihm folgen soll.

Walther

Warum ganz gleich?

Sachs

     Damit man seh',
ihr wähltet euch gleich ein Weib zur Eh'.

Walther (continues).

[2. Stolle]

20 "Wonnig entragend dem seligen Raum
     bot gold'ner Frucht
     heilsaft'ge Wucht

>mit holdem Prangen
>dem Verlangen
>an duft'ger Zweige Saum
>herrlich ein Baum."
>(He pauses.)

Sachs

5   Ihr schlosset nicht im gleichen Ton :
>das macht den Meistern Pein ;
doch nimmt Hans Sachs die Lehr' davon,
>im Lenz wohl müss' es so sein. —
Nun stellt mir einen Abgesang.

Walther

10   Was soll nun der?

Sachs

>Ob euch gelang
>ein rechtes Paar zu finden,
>das zeigt sich jetzt an den Kinden.
Den Stollen ähnlich, doch nicht gleich,
15   an eig'nen Reim' und Tönen reich;
dass man es recht schlank und selbstig find',
das freut die Eltern an dem Kind :
und euren Stollen gibt's den Schluss,
dass nichts davon abfallen muss.

Walther (continuing).

[Abgesang]

20   "Sei euch vertraut
>welch' hehres Wunder mir gescheh'n :
an meiner Seite stand ein Weib,
so schön und hold ich nie geseh'n;
>gleich einer Braut
25   umfasste sie sanft meinen Leib ;
>mit Augen winkend,
>die Hand wies blinkend,
was ich verlangend begehrt,
die Frucht so hold und wert
30   vom Lebensbaum."

Sachs (concealing his emotion).

Dass nenn' ich mir einen Abgesang :
seht, wie der ganze Bar gelang !

16. **dass** = *wenn.*

nur mit der Melodei
seid ihr ein wenig frei;
doch sag' ich nicht, dass es ein Fehler sei;
nur ist's nicht leicht zu behalten,
5   und das ärgert unsre Alten! —
Jetzt richtet mir noch einen zweiten Bar,
damit man merk' welch' der erste war.
Auch weiss ich noch nicht, so gut ihr's gereimt,
was ihr gedichtet, was ihr geträumt.

2. Gesätz

Walther (as before).

[1. Stolle]

10 "Abendlich glühend in himmlischer **Pracht**
verschied der Tag,
wie dort ich lag;
aus ihren Augen
Wonne zu saugen,
15   Verlangen einz'ger Macht
in mir nur wacht'. —

[2. Stolle]

Nächtlich umdämmert der Blick sich mir **bricht**!
wie weit so nah
beschienen da
20   zwei lichte Sterne
aus der Ferne
durch schlanker Zweige Licht
hehr mein Gesicht. —

[Abgesang]

Lieblich ein Quell
25 auf stiller Höhe dort mir rauscht;
jetzt schwellt er an sein hold Getön'
so süss und stark ich's nie erlauscht:
leuchtend und hell
wie strahlten die Sterne da schön;
30   zu Tanz und Reigen
in Laub und Zweigen
der gold'nen sammeln sich mehr,

15. **einz'ger Macht:** genitive absolute.   30. **Reigen** = *Reihen*.
32. **der gold'nen:** genitive with *Sternenheer*.

statt Frucht ein Sternenheer
im Lorbeerbaum." —

Sachs (deeply moved, softly).

Freund! eu'r Traumbild wies euch wahr:
gelungen ist auch der zweite Bar.
5 Wolltet ihr noch einen dritten dichten,
des Traumes Deutung würd' er berichten.

Walther

Wie fänd' ich die? Genug der Wort'!

Sachs (rising).

Dann Wort und Tat am rechten Ort! —
Drum bitt' ich, merkt mir gut die Weise;
10 gar lieblich drin sich's dichten lässt:
und singt ihr sie in weit'rem Kreise,
dann haltet mir auch das Traumbild fest.

Walther

Was habt ihr vor?

Sachs

Eu'r treuer Knecht
fand sich mit Sack und Tasch' zurecht;
15 die Kleider, drin am Hochzeitsfest
daheim bei euch ihr wolltet prangen,
die liess er her zu mir gelangen; —
ein Täubchen zeigt' ihm wohl das Nest,
darin sein Junker träumt':
20 drum folgt mir jetzt ins Kämmerlein!
Mit Kleiden, wohlgesäumt,
sollen beide wir gezieret sein,
wann's Stattliches zu wagen gilt: —
drum kommt, seid ihr gleich mir gewillt!

(He opens the door for *Walther* and goes in with him.)

Beckmesser

(peers into the shop; finding it empty, he comes in. He is richly
dressed but in a sad state. He limps, rubs and stretches, then twitches.
He seeks a stool and seats himself, but immediately springs up and
rubs himself again. Despairing and brooding he walks about; then
he pauses and peers through the window to the house opposite; makes
a gesture of anger; strikes his forehead with his hand. Finally his
eyes fall on the paper which *Sachs* has just written lying upon the

11. **Kreise**: "circle of Mastersingers." 21. **Kleiden** = *Kleidern.*

work-table. He picks it up curiously, reads it with hasty agitation
and finally breaks forth wrathfully):

Ein Werbelied ! Von Sachs ? — ist's wahr ?
Ah ! — Nun wird mir alles klar !

(Hearing the chamber door open, he starts up and hastily conceals the
sheet in his pocket.)

Sachs (in holiday attire, enters and stops).

Sieh da ! Herr Schreiber ? Auch am Morgen ?
Euch machen die Schuh' doch nicht mehr Sorgen ?
5 Lasst sehn ! mich dünkt, sie sitzen gut ?

Beckmesser

Den Teufel ! So dünn war ich noch nie beschuht :
fühl' durch die Sohle den feinsten Kies !

Sachs

Mein Merkersprüchlein wirkte dies :
trieb sie mit Merkerzeichen so weich.

Beckmesser

10 Schon gut der Witz' ! Und genug der Streich' !
Glaubt mir, Freund Sachs, jetzt kenn' ich euch ;
der Spass von dieser Nacht,
der wird euch noch gedacht :
dass ich euch nur nicht im Wege sei,
15 schuft ihr gar Aufruhr und Meuterei !

Sachs

's war Polterabend, lasst euch bedeuten :
eure Hochzeit spuckte unter den Leuten ;
je toller es da hergeh',
je besser bekommt's der Eh'.

Beckmesser (bursting forth).

20 O Schuster, voll von Ränken
und pöbelhaften Schwänken,
du war'st mein Feind von je :
nun hör' ob hell ich seh' !
Die ich mir auserkoren,
25 die ganz für mich geboren,
zu aller Witwer Schmach,
der Jungfer stellst du nach.
Dass sich Herr Sachs erwerbe
des Goldschmieds reiches Erbe,

17. **spuckte** = *spukte.*

im Meister-Rat zur Hand
auf Klauseln er bestand,
ein Mägdlein zu betören,
das nur auf ihn sollt' hören,
und, and'ren abgewandt,
zu ihm allein sich fand.
       Darum! darum —
       wär' ich so dumm? —
mit Schreien und mit Klopfen
wollt' er mein Lied zustopfen,
dass nicht dem Kind werd' kund
wie auch ein and'rer bestund!
       Ja ja! — Ha ha!
       Hab' ich dich da?
Aus seiner Schuster-Stuben
hetzt' endlich er den Buben
mit Knüppeln auf mich her,
dass meiner los er wär'!
       Au au! Au au!
       Wohl grün und blau,
zum Spott der allerliebsten Frau,
zerschlagen und zerprügelt,
dass kein Schneider mich auf bügelt!
       Gar auf mein Leben
       war's angegeben!
Doch kam ich noch so davon,
dass ich die Tat euch lohn'!
zieht heut' nur aus zum Singen,
merkt auf, wie's mag gelingen;
       bin ich gezwackt
       auch und zerhackt,
euch bring' ich doch sicher aus dem Takt!

Sachs

Gut Freund, ihr seid in argem Wahn!
Glaubt was ihr wollt, dass ich's getan,
gebt eure Eifersucht nur hin;
zu werben kommt mir nicht in Sinn.

Beckmesser

Lug und Trug! Ich weiss es besser.

12. bestund: see *bestehen*.   37. Lug und Trug: see *Lug*.

Sachs

Was fällt euch nur ein, Meister Beckmesser?
Was ich sonst im Sinn, geht euch nichts an:
doch glaubt, ob der Werbung seid ihr im Wahn.

Beckmesser

Ihr säng't heut' nicht?

Sachs

Nicht zur Wette.

Beckmesser

5 Kein Werbelied?

Sachs

Gewisslich, nein!

Beckmesser

Wenn ich aber drob ein Zeugnis hätte?

Sachs (looks on the work-table).

Das Gedicht? Hier liess ich's: — stecktet ihr's ein?

Beckmesser (produces the paper).

Ist das eure Hand?

Sachs

Ja, — war es das?

Beckmesser

Ganz frisch noch die Schrift?

Sachs

Und die Dinte noch nass!

Beckmesser

10 's wär' wohl gar ein biblisches Lied?

Sachs

Der fehlte wohl, wer darauf riet.

Beckmesser

Nun denn?

Sachs

Wie doch?

Beckmesser

Ihr fragt?

Sachs

Was noch?

Beckmesser

Dass ihr mit aller Biederkeit
der ärgste aller Spitzbuben seid !

Sachs

Mag sein ! Doch hab' ich noch nie entwandt,
was ich auf fremden Tischen fand : —
und dass man von euch auch nichts Übles denkt,
behaltet das Blatt, es sei euch geschenkt.

Beckmesser (springing up in joyful surprise).

Herr Gott !... Ein Gedicht !... Ein Gedicht von Sachs ?...
Doch halt', dass kein neuer Schad' mir erwachs' ! —
Ihr habt's wohl schon recht gut memoriert ?

Sachs

Seid meinethalb doch nur unbeirrt !

Beckmesser

Ihr lasst mir das Blatt ?

Sachs

Damit ihr kein Dieb.

Beckmesser

Und mach' ich Gebrauch ?

Sachs

Wie's euch belieb'.

Beckmesser

Doch, sing' ich das Lied ?

Sachs

Wenn's nicht zu schwer.

Beckmesser

Und wenn ich gefiel' ?

Sachs

Das wunderte mich sehr !

Beckmesser (quite familiarly).

Da seid ihr nun wieder zu bescheiden :
ein Lied von Sachs, das will 'was bedeuten !
Und seht, wie mir's ergeht,
wie's mit mir Armen steht !

16. 'was = etwas.

Erseh' ich doch mit Schmerzen,
mein Lied, das nachts ich sang, —
Dank euren lust'gen Scherzen! —
es machte der Pognerin bang.
Wie schaff' ich nun zur Stelle
ein neues Lied herzu?
Ich armer, zerschlag'ner Geselle,
wie fänd' ich heut' dazu Ruh'?
Werbung und ehlich Leben,
ob das mir Gott beschied,
muss ich nur grad' aufgeben,
hab' ich kein neues Lied.
Ein Lied von euch, dess'bin ich gewiss,
mit dem besieg' ich jed' Hindernis!
Soll ich das heute haben,
vergessen und begraben
sei Zwist, Hader und Streit,
und was uns je entzweit.

(He glances furtively at the paper; suddenly he frowns.)

Und doch! Wenn's nur eine Falle wär'! —
Noch gestern war't ihr mein Feind:
wie käm's, dass nach so grosser Beschwer'
ihr's freundlich heut' mit mir meint'?

Sachs

Ich machte euch Schuh' in später Nacht:
hat man so je einen Feind bedacht?

Beckmesser

Ja ja! recht gut! — doch eines schwört:
wo und wie ihr das Lied auch hört,
dass nie ihr euch beikommen lass't,
zu sagen, es sei von euch verfasst.

Sachs

Das schwör' ich und gelob' euch hier,
nie mich zu rühmen, das Lied sei von mir.

Beckmesser (joyously).

Was will ich mehr, ich bin geborgen!
Jetzt hat sich Beckmesser nicht mehr zu sorgen!

(He rubs his hands gleefully.)

Sachs

Doch, Freund, ich führ's euch zu Gemüte,
und rate euch in aller Güte :
      studiert mir recht das Lied!
      Sein Vortrag ist nicht leicht :
5   ob euch die Weise geriet',
      und ihr den Ton erreicht '

Beckmesser

Freund Sachs, ihr seid ein guter Poet ;
doch was Ton und Weise betrifft, gesteht,
      da tut's mir keiner vor !
10   Drum spitzt nur fein das Ohr,
        und : Beckmesser,
        keiner besser !
      Darauf macht euch gefasst,
      wenn ihr ruhig mich singen lasst. —
15   Doch nun memorieren,
      schnell nach Haus !
      Ohne Zeit verlieren
      richt' ich das aus. —
      Hans Sachs, mein Teurer !
20   ich hab' euch verkannt :
      durch den Abenteurer
      war ich verrannt :
      so einer fehlte uns blos !
      Den wurden wir Meister doch los !
25   Doch mein Besinnen
      läuft mir von hinnen :
      bin ich verwirrt,
      und ganz verirrt ?
      Die Silben, die Reime,
30   die Worte, die Verse :
      ich kleb' wie an Leime,
      und brennt doch die Ferse
      Ade ! ich muss fort !
      An andrem Ort
35   dank' ich euch inniglich,
      weil ihr so minniglich ;

---

1. **führ's:** see *führen*. 5. **geriet** = *gelang*. 21. **Abenteurer** =
Walther.

für euch nun stimme ich,
kauf' eure Werke gleich,
mache zum Merker euch:
doch fein mit Kreide weich,
5   nicht mit dem Hammerstreich!
Merker! Merker! Merker Hans Sachs!
das Nürnberg schusterlich blüh' und wachs'!
(He limps, stumbles and totters away as if possessed.)

Sachs

So ganz boshaft doch keinen ich fand,
er hält's auf die Länge nicht aus:
10 vergeudet mancher oft viel Verstand,
doch hält er auch damit Haus:
die schwache Stunde kommt für jeden;
da wird er dumm, und lässt mit sich reden.
Dass hier Herr Beckmesser ward zum Dieb,
15 ist mir für meinen Plan sehr lieb. —
(Through the window he sees *Eva* coming.)
Sieh' Evchen! Dacht' ich doch wo sie blieb'!
(*Eva*, in a white dress with many ornaments, steps into the shop.)

Sachs

Grüss' Gott, mein Evchen! Ei, wie herrlich,
wie stolz du's heute meinst!
Du machst wohl Jung und Alt begehrlich
20 wenn du so schön erscheinst.

Eva

Meister! 's ist nicht so gefährlich:
und ist's dem Schneider geglückt,
wer sieht dann an wo's mir beschwerlich,
wo still der Schuh mich drückt?

Sachs

25 Der böse Schuh! 's war deine Laun'
dass du ihn gestern nicht probiert.

Eva

Merk' wohl, ich hatt' zu viel Vertrau'n
im Meister hab' ich mich geirrt.

11. **hält**: see *halten*. 12. **reden**: see *reden*.

Sachs

Ei, 's tut mir leid! Zeig' her, mein Kind,
dass ich dir helfe, gleich geschwind.

Eva

Sobald ich stehe, will es geh'n :
doch will ich geh'n, zwingt's mich zu steh'n.

Sachs

5 Hier auf den Schemel streck' den Fuss :
der üblen Not ich wehren muss.

(She puts her foot on the stool by the work-table.)

Was ist's mit dem ?

Eva

Ihr seht, zu weit!

Sachs

Kind, das ist pure Eitelkeit :
der Schuh ist knapp.

Eva

Das sag' ich ja :
10 drum drückt er mir die Zehen da.

Sachs

Hier links ?

Eva

Nein, rechts.

Sachs

Wohl mehr am Spann ?

Eva

Mehr hier am Hacken.

Sachs

Kommt der auch dran ?

Eva

Ach Meister! Wüsstet ihr besser als ich,
wo der Schuh mich drückt ?

Sachs

Ei, 's wundert mich
15 dass er zu weit, und doch drückt überall ?

Walther, in glittering knightly apparel, enters from the chamber
door, but stops spell-bound at the sight of *Eva*, who utters a slight

cry, and likewise remains in her position with one foot upon the stool.
Sachs, kneeling before her, has his back turned to the door.

Aha! hier sitzt's! Nun begreif' ich den Fall!
Kind, du hast recht: 's stack in der Naht: —
nun warte, dem Übel schaff' ich Rat.
Bleib' nur so stehn; ich nehm' dir den Schuh
5 eine Weil' auf den Leisten: dann lässt er dir Ruh'!

(He has gently drawn the shoe from her foot, and, while she remains
in this position, *Sachs* pretends to busy himself, and acts as though
he noticed nothing.)

Sachs (while at work).

Immer Schustern! das ist nun mein Los;
des Nachts, des Tags — komm' nicht davon los! —
Kind, hör' zu! Ich hab's überdacht,
was meinem Schustern ein Ende macht:
10 am besten, ich werbe doch noch um dich;
da gewänn ich doch 'was als Poet für mich! —
Du hörst nicht drauf? — So sprich doch jetzt!
Hast mir's ja selbst in den Kopf gesetzt? —
Schon gut! — ich merk'! — Mach' deinen Schuh!...
15 Säng' mir nur wenigstens einer dazu!
Hörte heut' gar ein schönes Lied: —
wem dazu ein dritter Vers geriet'!

3. GESÄTZ

Walther (still in the same position, opposite *Eva*).
[1. Stolle]

"Weilten die Sterne im lieblichen Tanz?
So licht und klar
20 im Lockenhaar,
vor allen Frauen
hehr zu schauen,
lag ihr mit zartem Glanz
ein Sternenkranz. —

[2. Stolle]

25 Wunder ob Wunder nun bieten sich dar:
zwiefachen Tag
ich grüssen mag;
denn gleich zwei'n Sonnen
reinster Wonnen,
30 der hehrsten Augen Paar
nahm ich nun wahr. —

[Abgesang]

Huldreichstes Bild,
dem ich zu nahen mich erkühnt :
den Kranz, vor zweier Sonnen Strahl
zugleich verblichen und ergrünt,
5   minnig und mild,
        sie flocht ihn ums Haupt dem Gemahl.
        Dort Huld-geboren,
        nun Ruhm-erkoren,
      giesst paradiesische Lust
10   sie in des Dichters Brust —
        im Liebestraum.” —

Sachs

(busily at work, brings back the shoe and fits it to *Eva's* foot during
the last verse of *Walther's* song).

Lausch’ Kind ! das ist ein Meisterlied :
derlei hörst du jetzt bei mir singen.
Nun schau’, ob dabei mein Schuh geriet ?
15   Mein’ endlich doch
          es tät’ mir gelingen ?
Versuch’s ! tritt auf ! — Sag’, drückt er dich noch ?

(*Eva*, motionless as if enchanted, gazes and listens. She now breaks
forth in violent sobbing, and sinks on *Sachs's* breast weeping and cling-
ing to him. *Walther* steps up to them and wrings *Sachs's* hand with
enthusiasm. *Sachs* composes himself with effort, tears himself away,
and lets *Eva* rest unconsciously on *Walther's* shoulder.)

Sachs

Hat man mit dem Schuhwerk nicht seine Not !
Wär’ ich nicht noch Poet dazu,
20 ich machte länger keine Schuh’ !
Das ist eine Müh’ und Aufgebot !
Zu weit dem einen, dem andern zu eng ;
Von allen Seiten Luft und Gedräng’ :
          da klappt’s,
25   da schlappt’s,
          hier drückt’s,
          da zwickt’s !
Der Schuster soll auch alles wissen,
flicken was nur immer zerrissen ;
30 und ist er nun Poet dazu,

6. **ihn** = *Kranz.*

so lässt man am End' ihm auch da kein' Ruh':
doch ist er erst noch Witwer gar,
zum Narren macht man ihn fürwahr;
die jüngsten Mädchen, ist Not am Mann,
5 begehren, er hielte um sie an;
versteht er sie, versteht er sie nicht,
alleins ob ja, ob nein er spricht:
am Ende riecht er doch nach Pech,
und gilt für dumm, tückisch und frech!
10 Ei, 's ist mir nur um den Lehrbuben leid;
        der verliert mir allen Respekt;
die Lene macht ihn schon nicht recht gescheit,
        dass in Töpf' und Tellern er leckt!
Wo Teufel er jetzt wieder steckt?

    (He acts as though he were seeking for *David*.)

    Eva (holds *Sachs* and draws him to her again).

15 O Sachs! mein Freund! Mein teurer Mann!
Wie ich dir Edlem lohnen kann!
        Was ohne deine Liebe,
        was wär' ich ohne dich,
        ob je auch Kind ich bliebe,
20   erwecktest du nicht mich?
            Durch dich gewann ich
            was man preist,
            durch dich ersann ich
            was ein Geist!
25   Durch dich erwacht,
            durch dich nur dacht'
        ich edel, frei und kühn:
        du liessest mich erblüh'n! —
O lieber Meister! schilt mich nur!
30 Ich war doch auf der rechten Spur:
        denn, hatte ich die Wahl,
        nur dich erwählt' ich mir:
        du warest mein Gemahl,
        den Preis nur reicht' ich dir! —
35   Doch nun hat's mich gewählt
        zu nie gekannter Qual:
        und werd' ich heut' vermählt,
        so war's ohn' alle Wahl!

Das war ein Müssen, war ein Zwang!
Dir selbst, mein Meister, wurde bang.

Sachs

      Mein Kind:
   von Tristan und Isolde
5   kenn' ich ein traurig Stück:
   Hans war klug, und wollte
   nichts von Herrn Markes Glück. —
'S war Zeit, dass ich den Rechten erkannt:
wär' sonst am End' doch hineingerannt! —
10 Aha! da streicht schon die Lene ums Haus.
Nur herein! — He, David! Kommst nicht heraus?

(*Magdalene*, in holiday attire, enters the shop door; *David* appears in
the chamber door at the same time, likewise gaily dressed, and decked
out in ribbons and flowers.)

Die Zeugen sind da, Gevatter zur Hand
jetzt schnell zur Taufe; nehmt euren Stand!

(All look at him with surprise.)

    Ein Kind ward hier geboren;
15 jetzt sei ihm ein Nam' erkoren!
So ist's nach Meister-Weis' und Art,
wenn eine Meisterweise geschaffen ward:
dass die einen guten Namen trag',
dran jeder sie erkennen mag. —
20   Vernehmt respektable Gesellschaft,
was euch hierher zur Stell' schafft! —
Eine Meisterweise ist gelungen,
von Junker Walther gedichtet und gesungen;
der jungen Weise lebender Vater
25 'lud mich und die Pognerin zum Gevatter:
weil wir die Weise wohl vernommen,
sind wir zur Taufe hierher gekommen.
Auch dass wir zur Handlung Zeugen haben,
ruf' ich Jungfer Lene, und meinen Knaben:
30 doch da's zum Zeugen kein Lehrbube tut,
und heut' auch den Spruch er gesungen gut,

4. **Tristan und Isolde:** an old Celtic myth, popular during the
middle ages, upon which Wagner bases one of his music dramas.
Isolde, betrothed to old King Mark, to whom Sachs compares himself
in this passage, falls in love with the young knight Tristan and a
tragedy follows.

so mach' ich den Burschen gleich zum Gesell';
knie' nieder, David, und nimm diese Schell'!

(David kneels, and *Sachs* gives him a sharp blow on the ear.)

Steh' auf, Gesell! und denk an den Streich;
du merkst dir dabei die Taufe zugleich! —
5 Fehlt sonst noch 'was, uns keiner drum schilt:
wer weiss, ob's nicht gar einer Nottaufe gilt.
Dass die Weise Kraft behalte zum Leben,
will ich nur gleich den Namen ihr geben: —
"die selige Morgentraumdeut-Weise"
10 sei sie genannt zu des Meisters Preise. —
Nun wachse sie gross, ohn' Schad' und Bruch:
die jüngste Gevatterin spricht den Spruch.

Eva

Selig, wie die Sonne
meines Glückes lacht,
15 Morgen voller Wonne,
selig mir erwacht!
Traum der höchsten Hulden,
himmlisch Morgenglüh'n!
Deutung euch zu schulden,
20 selig süss Bemüh'n!
Einer Weise mild und hehr,
sollt' es hold gelingen,
meines Herzens süss Beschwer
deutend zu bezwingen.
25 Ob es nur ein Morgentraum?
Selig deut' ich mir es kaum.
Doch die Weise,
was sie leise
mir vertraut
30 im stillen Raum,
hell und laut,
in der Meister vollem Kreis,
deute sie den höchsten Preis!

Walther

35 Deine Liebe, rein und hehr'
liess es mir gelingen,
meines Herzens süss Beschwer
deutend zu bezwingen.

Ob es noch der Morgentraum?
Selig deut' ich mir es kaum.
   Doch die Weise,
   was sie leise
   dir vertraut
   im stillen Raum,
   hell und laut,
in der Meister vollem Kreis,
werbe sie um höchsten Preis!

Sachs

Vor dem Kinde lieblich hehr,
   mocht' ich gern wohl singen;
doch des Herzens süss Beschwer
   galt es zu bezwingen.
'S war ein schöner Abendtraum:
daran zu deuten wag' ich kaum.
   Diese Weise,
   was sie leise
   mir vertraut
   im stillen Raum,
   sagt mir laut:
auch der Jugend ew'ges Reis
grünt nur durch des Dichters Preis.

David

Wach' oder träum' ich schon so früh?
Das zu erklären macht mir Müh'.
's ist wohl nur ein Morgentraum:
was ich seh', begreif' ich kaum.
   Ward zur Stelle
   gleich Geselle?
   Lene Braut?
   Im Kirchenraum
   wir getraut?
's geht der Kopf mir, wie im Kreis,
dass ich bald gar Meister heiss'!

Magdalene

Wach' oder träum' ich schon so früh?
Das zu erklären macht mir Müh':
's ist wohl nur ein Morgentraum?
Was ich seh', begreif' ich kaum!

Er zur Stelle
gleich Geselle?
Ich die Braut?
Im Kirchenraum
5 wir getraut?
Ja, wahrhaftig! 's geht: wer weiss?
Bald ich wohl Frau Meist'rin heiss'!

The orchestra begins to play softly a merry march-like theme.
Sachs disperses the groups.

Sachs

Jetzt all' am Fleck! Den Vater grüss'!
Auf, nach der Wies' schnell auf die Füss'!

(*Eva* breaks away from *Walther* and *Sachs*, and leaves the work-room
with *Magdalene*.)

10 Nun, Junker! Kommt! Habt frohen Mut! —
David, Gesell'! Schliess' den Laden gut!

As *Sachs* and *Walther* likewise go into the street, and *David* is
left shutting the shop doors, curtains are drawn from each side of the
proscenium, so that the whole stage is concealed. Later, as the music
comes to a climax, the curtains rise, revealing a changed scene.

VERWANDLUNG

The scene now presents an open meadow. In the far background
the city of Nuremberg. The Pegnitz winds across the meadow. The
narrow river is as far forward as possible. Boats with flags fluttering
are continually landing parties of gaily dressed citizens, members of
the different guilds, with their wives and children, all of whom land
on the bank at the place of the festival. An elevated stage with benches,
erected at the right, is already decorated with the flags of those who
have come. The standard-bearers of the freshly arriving guilds
also place their flags about the singer's stage, so that it is eventually
closed up by them on three sides. Tents furnishing drinks and re-
freshments of all sorts border the sides of the foreground.

There is much merry-making before the tents. Citizens with their
wives and families are grouped about there. The *Apprentices* of the
Mastersingers, gaily dressed and adorned with ribbons and flowers,
each one carrying a slender ornamental wand, merrily perform the
office of ushers and heralds. They receive the new arrivals on the

bank, arrange the marching order of the guilds, and escort them to
the singer's stage, whence, after the standard bearers have planted
their banners, the citizen members and journeymen disperse freely
among the tents.

Among the guilds arriving, the following are especially prominent.

Die Schuster (as they go by).

> Sankt Crispin,
> lobet ihn!
> War gar ein heilig Mann,
> zeigt was ein Schuster kann.
> Die Armen hatten gute Zeit,
> macht' ihnen warme Schuh';
> und wenn ihm keiner Leder leiht,
> so stahl er sich's dazu.
> Der Schuster hat ein weit Gewissen,
> macht Schuhe selbst mit Hindernissen;
> und ist vom Gerber das Fell erst weg,
> dann streck'! streck'! streck'!
> Leder taugt nur am rechten Fleck.

The town-pipers and toy-instrument-makers march by, playing on
their different instruments. Following these are

Die Schneider

> Als Nürenberg belagert war,
> und Hungersnot sich fand,
> wär' Stadt und Volk verdorben gar,
> war nicht ein Schneider zur Hand,
> der Mut hat und Verstand:
> hat sich in ein Bockfell eingenäht,
> auf dem Stadtwall da spazieren geht,
> und macht wohl seine Sprünge
> gar lustig guter Dinge.
> Der Feind, der sieht's und zieht vom Fleck:
> der Teufel hol' die Stadt sich weg,
> hat's drin noch so lustige Meck-meck-meck!
> Meck! Meck! Meck!
> Wer glaubt's, dass ein Schneider im Bocke steck'!

(Imitating the bleating of a goat.)

---

1. **St. Crispin:** the patron saint of the "gentle craft" of shoe-
making. 13. **Leder...Fleck:** a plausible reason for the theft. 27. **Wer
...steck':** in popular shows to-day the tailor often makes up to resemble a goat and the other characters cry "Meck! Meck!" at him.

Die Bäcker

(marching close behind the tailors, so that the songs of the two guilds are mingled).

Hungersnot!   Hungersnot!
  Das ist ein greulich Leiden!
Gäb' euch der Bäcker kein täglich Brot,
  müsst' alle Welt verscheiden.
5   Beck!   Beck!   Beck!
  Täglich auf dem Fleck!
  Nimm uns den Hunger weg!

Lehrbuben

Herr je!   Herr je!   Mädel von Fürth!
Stadtpfeifer, spielt!   dass 's lustig wird!

A gaily painted boat, occupied by young girls in rich peasant costume, arrives. The *Apprentices* lift the girls out and dance with them, while the town-piper plays in the foreground. The object of this dance is to bring the girls to the front of the stage. But this arrangement is somewhat delayed by the efforts of the journeymen to capture the girls, who, to escape their pursuers, complete, together with their partners, the entire circuit of the stage.

The whole scene is one of fun and frolic.

David (coming forward from the landing place).

10 Ihr tanzt?   Was werden die Meister sagen?

(The boys make faces at him.)

Hört nicht? — Lass' ich mir's auch behagen!

(He seizes a young and pretty girl and begins to dance with her with great vigor. The spectators laugh and enjoy it.)

Ein paar Lehrbuben

David!   die Lene!   die Lene sieht zu!

David (frightened, lets the girl go, but seeing nothing, takes courage and dances more wildly than ever).

Ach!   lasst mich mit euren Possen in Ruh'!

Gesellen (at the landing place).

Die Meistersinger!   die Meistersinger!

David

15 Herr Gott! — Ade, ihr hübschen Dinger!

He gives the girl an ardent kiss and tears himself away. The *Apprentices* quickly cease their dancing, hasten to the bank and line up to receive the *Mastersingers*. At the command of the *Apprentices* all stand back. The *Mastersingers* form into line at the landing and then march away to take their places on the elevated platform. First comes *Kothner* as standard-bearer; then *Pogner* leading *Eva* by the hand, who is accompanied by gaily adorned maidens among whom is *Magdalene*. Then follow the other *Mastersingers*, who are greeted by waving of hats and cheers. When they have all reached the stage, *Eva*, surrounded by the maidens, takes the seat of honor, and when *Kothner* has planted his banner in the middle of the others, so that it towers above them all, the *Apprentices* solemnly advance in rank and file turning toward the people.

Lehrbuben

Silentium!   Silentium!
Lasst all' Reden und Gesumm'!

Sachs rises and steps forward. At the sight of him all unite in shouts of joy and wave their hats and handkerchiefs.

Alles Volk.

Ha! Sachs! 's ist Sachs!
Seht!   Meister Sachs!
5   Stimmt an!   Stimmt an!   Stimmt an!
(With dignified delivery.)
"Wach' auf, es nahet gen den Tag,
"ich hör' singen im grünen Hag
"ein wonnigliche Nachtigal,
"ihr Stimm' durchklinget Berg und Tal:
10   "die Nacht neigt sich zum Occident,
"der Tag geht auf von Orient,
"die rotbrünstige Morgenröt'
"her durch die trüben Wolken geht." —
Heil Sachs!   Hans Sachs!
15   Heil Nürnbergs teurem Sachs!

Long silence of deep emotion. *Sachs*, who, motionless as if pre-occupied, has been gazing away over the crowd of people, finally looks at them kindly, bows pleasantly and begins to speak at first with emotion, but soon with increasing firmness.

Sachs

Euch wird es leicht, mir macht ihr's schwer,
gebt ihr mir Armen zu viel Ehr':
such' vor der Ehr' ich zu besteh'n,
sei's, mich von euch geliebt zu seh'n!
20   Schon grosse Ehr' ward mir erkannt,
ward heut' ich zum Spruchsprecher ernannt:
und was mein Spruch euch künden soll,

6. **gen** = gegen.

glaubt, das ist hoher Ehre voll !
Wenn ihr die Kunst so hoch schon ehrt,
    da galt es zu beweisen,
dass, wer ihr selbst gar angehört,
5   sie schätzt ob allen Preisen.
Ein Meister, reich und hochgemut,
    der will euch heut' das zeigen :
sein Töchterlein, sein höchstes Gut,
    mit allem Hab und Eigen,
10 dem Singer, der im Kunstgesang
vor allem Volk den Preis errang ;
    als höchsten Preises Kron'
    er bietet das zum Lohn.
Darum so hört, und stimmet bei :
15 die Werbung steht dem Dichter frei.
Ihr Meister, die ihr's euch getraut,
euch ruf' ich's vor dem Volke laut :
erwägt der Werbung selt'nen Preis,
    und wem sie soll gelingen,
20 dass er sich rein und edel weiss,
    im Werben, wie im Singen,
    will er das Reis erringen,
das nie bei neuen, noch bei alten
ward je so herrlich hoch gehalten,
25   als von der lieblich Reinen,
    die niemals soll beweinen,
dass Nürenberg mit höchstem Wert
die Kunst und ihre Meister ehrt.

Great commotion. *Sachs* goes up to *Pogner*, who, deeply stirred, presses his hand.

Pogner

O Sachs ! Mein Freund ! Wie dankenswert !
30 Wie wisst ihr, was mein Herz beschwert !

Sachs

's war viel gewagt ! Jetzt habt nur Mut !

(He turns to *Beckmesser*, who during the preceding events and since has constantly been taking the manuscript secretly out of his pocket, and in his vain endeavor to commit it to memory often despairingly wipes the sweat from his brow.)

Herr Merker ! Sagt, wie steht es ? Gut ?

16. **die ihr's** = *ihr die es.*

Beckmesser

O, dieses Lied ! — Werd' nicht draus klug,
und hab' doch dran studiert genug !

Sachs

Mein Freund, 's ist euch nicht aufgezwungen.

Beckmesser

Was hilft's ? — Mit dem meinen ist doch versungen !
5 's war eure Schuld ! — Jetzt seid hübsch für mich !
's wär' schändlich, liesset ihr mich im Stich !

Sachs

Ich dächt', ihr gäbt's auf.

Beckmesser

Warum nicht gar ?
Die andren sing' ich alle zu paar' !
Wenn ihr nur nicht singt.

Sachs

So seht, wie's geht !

Beckmesser

10 Das Lied ! — bin's sicher — zwar keiner versteht :
doch bau' ich auf eure Popularität.

The *Apprentices* have hastily made a little mound of turf before
the platform of the *Mastersingers*, stamped it firmly, and decorated it
with flowers.

Sachs

Nun denn, wenn's Meistern und Volk beliebt,
Zum Wettgesang man den Anfang gibt.

Kothner (coming forward).

Ihr ledig' Meister, macht euch bereit !
15 Der ältest' sich zuerst anlässt : —
Herr Beckmesser, ihr fangt an, 's ist Zeit !

Beckmesser

(leaves the platform. The *Apprentices* conduct him to the mound, he
stumbles, walks unevenly and totters).

Zum Teufel ! Wie wackelig ! Macht das hübsch fest !
(The boys snicker, and stamp the earth down again.)

6. **liesset:** see *lassen*.   8. **sing':** see *singen*.

Das Volk

(to one another while *Beckmesser* is getting ready).

Wie, der? Der wirbt? Scheint mir nicht der Rechte!
An der Tochter Stell' ich den nicht möchte. —
    Er kann nicht 'mal stehn :
    Wie wird's mit dem gehn? —
5 Seid still! 's ist gar ein tücht'ger Meister!
Stadtschreiber ist er : Beckmesser heisst er. —
    Gott! ist der dumm!
    Er fällt fast um! —
Still! macht keinen Witz ;
10 der hat im Rate Stimm und Sitz.

Die Lehrbuben (drawn up in a row).

Silentium! Silentium!
Lasst all das Reden und Gesumm'!

Beckmesser, makes an exaggerated bow to *Eva*, all the while watching the expression of her face.

Kothner

Fanget an!

Beckmesser

(sings his own melody, the text of which is an awful, though unintentional, caricature of *Walther's* song. His ornamental phrases are continually spoiled by his lapses of memory and his increasing confusion).

"Morgen ich leuchte in rosigem Schein,
    voll Blut und Duft
15   geht schnell die Luft; —
    wohl bald gewonnen!
    wie zerronnen, —
im Garten lud ich ein —
    garstig und fein." —

Die Meister (softly to one another).

20 Mein! was ist das? Ist er von Sinnen?
Woher mocht' er solche Gedanken gewinnen?

Volk (likewise).

Sonderbar! Hört ihr's? Wen lud er ein?
Verstand man recht? Wie kann das sein?

3. **'mal**: see *einmal.* 16. **wohl...zerronnen**: in his confusion Beckmesser mistakes an old proverb. His entire performance is simply incoherent nonsense; for its utter perversion of the meaning, compare Walther's song on p. 103 line for line.

Beckmesser

(after he has got a firm footing and peeped secretly into the manuscript).

"Wohn' ich erträglich im selbigen Raum,
　　hol' Gold und Frucht —
　　Bleisaft und Wucht :
　　mich holt am Pranger —
　　der Verlanger, —
5　　auf luft'ger Steige kaum —
　　häng' ich am Baum." —

(He seeks to steady himself and find his place in the manuscript.)

Die Meister

Was soll das heissen ?　Ist er nur toll ?
Sein Lied ist ganz von Unsinn voll !

Das Volk (louder).

10　Schöner Werber !　Der find't seinen Lohn :
bald hängt er am Galgen ; man sieht ihn schon.

Beckmesser (getting more and more confused).

"Heimlich mir graut —
weil hier es munter will hergeh'n :
an meiner Leiter stand ein Weib, —
15　sie schämt' und wollt' mich nicht beseh'n.
Bleich wie ein Kraut —
umfasert mir Hanf meinen Leib ; —
　　die Augen zwinkend —
　　der Hund blies winkend —
20　was ich vor langem verzehrt, —
wie Frucht, so Holz und Pferd —
　　vom Leberbaum." —

(Here all break out in unrestrained laughter.)

Beckmesser

(leaves the mound in a rage and hastens to *Sachs*).

Verdammter Schuster !　Das dank' ich dir !
Das Lied, es ist gar nicht von mir :
25　von Sachs, der hier so hoch verehrt,
von eu'rem Sachs ward mir's beschert !
Mich hat der Schändliche gedrängt,
sein schlechtes Lied mir aufgehängt.

(He rushes furiously away and is lost among the crowd.　Great confusion.)

Volk

Mein! Was soll das? Jetzt wird's immer bunter!
Von Sachs das Lied? Das nähm' uns doch Wunder!

Die Meistersinger

Erklärt doch, Sachs! Welch ein Skandal!
Von euch das Lied? Welch eig'ner Fall!

Sachs
(who has quietly picked up the manuscript which *Beckmesser* has
thrown at him).

5 Das Lied fürwahr ist nicht von mir:
Herr Beckmesser irrt, wie dort so hier!
Wie er dazu kam, mag er selbst sagen:
doch möcht' ich mich nie zu rühmen wagen,
ein Lied, so schön wie dies erdacht,
10 sei von mir, Hans Sachs, gemacht.

Meistersinger

Wie? schön dies Lied? Der Unsinn-Wust!

Volk

Hört, Sachs macht Spass! Er sagt's zur Lust.

Sachs

Ich sag' euch Herr'n, das Lied ist schön:
nur ist's auf den ersten Blick zu erseh'n,
15 dass Freund Beckmesser es entstellt.
Doch schwör' ich, dass es euch gefällt,
        wenn richtig die Wort' und Weise
        hier einer säng' im Kreise.
Und wer das verstünd', zugleich bewies',
20   dass er des Liedes Dichter,
und gar mit Rechte Meister hiess',
        fänd er geneigte Richter. —
Ich bin verklagt, und muss besteh'n:
drum lasst meinen Zeugen mich auserseh'n! —
25 Ist jemand hier, der recht mir weiss,
der tret' als Zeug' in diesen Kreis!

        (*Walther* advances from the crowd. General stir.)

So zeuget, das Lied sei nicht von mir;
und zeuget auch, dass, was ich hier

---

2. **Wunder**: see *Wunder*. 6. **wie dort so hier**: see *dort*. 19. **verstünd'**: from *verstehen*.

hab' von dem Lied gesagt,
zuviel nicht sei gewagt.

Die Meister

Ei, Sachs! Gesteht, ihr seid gar fein!
So mag's denn heut geschehen sein.

Sachs

5 Der Regel Güte daraus man erwägt,
dass sie auch 'mal 'ne Ausnahm' verträgt.

Das Volk

Ein guter Zeuge, schön und kühn!
Mich dünkt, dem kann 'was Gut's erblüh'n.

Sachs

Meister und Volk sind gewillt
10 zu vernehmen, was mein Zeuge gilt.
Herr Walter von Stolzing, singt das Lied!
Ihr Meister, les't, ob's ihm geriet.

(He gives the *Masters* the manuscript that they may follow him.)

Die Lehrbuben

Alles gespannt, 's gibt kein Gesumm',
da rufen wir auch nicht Silentium!

Walther
(who has stepped boldly and firmly upon the mound).

15 " Morgenlich leuchtend in rosigem Schein,
     von Blüt' und Duft
     geschwellt die Luft,
    voll aller Wonnen
    nie ersonnen,
20 ein Garten lud mich ein, —

(The *Masters*, touched by the song, let the manuscript fall. *Walther*
notices it, without seeming to do so, and now proceeds more freely.)

dort unter einem Wunderbaum,
    von Früchten reich behangen,
zu schau'n in sel'gem Liebestraum,
    was höchstem Lustverlangen
25   Erfüllung kühn verhiess —
     das schönste Weib,
    Eva im Paradies."

Das Volk (softly to one another).

Das ist 'was and'res! Wer hätt's gedacht?
Was doch recht Wort und Vortrag macht!

Die Meistersinger (softly aside).

Ja wohl! Ich merk'! 's ist ein ander Ding,
ob falsch man oder richtig sing'.

Sachs

5   Zeuge am Ort!
    Fahret fort!

Walther

"Abendlich dämmernd umschloss mich die Nacht;
    auf steilem Pfad
    war ich genaht
10   wohl einer Quelle
    edler Welle,
  die lockend mir gelacht:
dort unter einem Lorbeerbaum,
  von Sternen hell durchschienen,
15 ich schaut' im wachen Dichtertraum,
  mit heilig holden Mienen
  mich netzend mit dem Nass,
   das hehrste Weib —
  die Muse des Parnass."

Das Volk (more softly, aside).

20 So hold und traut, wie fern es schwebt,
doch ist's als ob man's mit erlebt!

Die Meistersinger

's ist kühn und seltsam, das ist wahr:
doch wohlgereimt und singebar.

Sachs

Zum dritten, Zeuge wohl erkiest!
25 Fahret fort, und schliesst!

Walther (with enthusiastic inspiration).

  "Huldreichster Tag,
dem ich aus Dichters Traum erwacht!
Das ich geträumt, das Paradies,

24. erkiest: from *erküren* (*erkiesen*).

in himmlisch neu verklärter Pracht
hell vor mir lag,
dahin der Quell lachend mich wies :
die, dort geboren,
mein Herz erkoren,
der Erde lieblichstes Bild,
zur Muse mir geweiht,
so heilig hehr als mild,
ward kühn von mir gefreit,
am lichten Tag der Sonnen
durch Sanges Sieg gewonnen
Parnass und Paradies !"

Volk (softly joining in at the close).

Gewiegt wie in den schönsten Traum,
hör' ich es wohl, doch fass' es kaum.
Reich' ihm das Reis
Sein der Preis !
keiner wie er zu werben weiss !

Die Meister

Ja, holder Sänger !   Nimm das Reis !
Dein Sang erwarb dir Meisterpreis !

Pogner

O Sachs !   Dir dank' ich Glück und Ehr' !
Vorüber nun all' Herzbeschwer !

Eva, who from the beginning of the scene has maintained a calm,
undisturbed manner, seemingly oblivious to all that has been going on,
has listened to *Walther* immovably; now, at the end of the song when
both Masters and people, deeply stirred, involuntarily express their admiration, she rises, steps to the edge of the platform and places on the
head of *Walther*, who is kneeling on the step, a wreath of laurel and
myrtle. whereupon he rises and is led by her to her father, before
whom they kneel together. *Pogner* extends his hands over them blessing them.

Sachs (pointing out the couple to the people).

Den Zeugen, denk' es, wählt' ich gut ;
tragt ihr Hans Sachs drum üblen Mut ?

Volk (enthusiastically).

Hans Sachs !   Nein !   Das war schön erdacht !
Das habt ihr einmal wieder gut gemacht !

13. **gewiegt:** see *gewiegt.*

Mehrere Meistersinger.

Auf, Meister Pogner! Euch zum Ruhm,
meldet dem Junker sein Meistertum.

Pogner (bringing a golden chain with three medals).

Geschmückt mit König Davids Bild,
nehm' ich euch auf in der Meister Gild'.

Walther (starts back involuntarily).

5   Nicht Meister! Nein!
Will ohne Meister selig sein!

(The *Masters* look up to *Sachs* in consternation.)

Sachs (taking *Walther* firmly by the hand).

Verachtet mir die Meister nicht,
          und ehrt mir ihre Kunst!
Was ihnen hoch zum Lobe spricht,
10   fiel reichlich euch zur Gunst.
Nicht euren Ahnen, noch so wert,
nicht euren Wappen, Speer, noch Schwert,
          dass ihr ein Dichter seid,
          ein Meister euch gefreit,
15 dem dankt ihr heut' eu'r höchstes Glück.
Drum, denkt mit Dank ihr d'ran zurück,
wie kann die Kunst wohl unwert sein,
die solche Preise schliesset ein? —
Dass uns're Meister sie gepflegt,
20   grad' recht nach ihrer Art,
nach ihrem Sinne treu gehegt,
          das hat sie echt bewahrt:
blieb sie nicht adlig, wie zur Zeit,
wo Höf' und Fürsten sie geweiht,
25   im Drang der schlimmen Jahr'
          blieb sie doch deutsch und wahr;
und wär' sie anders nicht geglückt,
als wie wo alles drängt' und drückt',
ihr seht, wie hoch sie blieb in Ehr'!
30 Was wollt ihr von den Meistern mehr?
Habt acht! Uns drohen üble Streich': —
zerfällt erst deutsches Volk und Reich,
in falscher welscher Majestät
kein Fürst dann mehr sein Volk versteht;

und welschen Dunst mit welschem Tand
sie pflanzen uns ins deutsche Land.
Was deutsch und echt wüsst' keiner mehr,
lebt's nicht in deutscher Meister Ehr',
5   Drum sag' ich euch:
ehrt eure deutschen Meister:
dann bannt ihr gute Geister!
Und gebt ihr ihrem Wirken Gunst,
       zerging' in Dunst
10   das heil'ge röm'sche Reich,
      uns bliebe gleich
      die heil'ge deutsche Kunst!

All join fervently in the closing verse. *Eva* takes the crown from *Walther's* head and places it on *Sachs's*. The latter takes the chain from *Pogner's* hand, and hangs it round *Walther's* neck. *Walther* and *Eva* lean on *Sachs*, one on each side. *Pogner*, as if doing homage, falls on his knee before *Sachs*. The *Mastersingers* all point to *Sachs*, proclaiming him their chief. While the *Apprentices* shout, clap their hands and dance, the people wave their hats and handkerchiefs with enthusiasm.

Volk

Heil Sachs! Hans Sachs!
Heil Nürnbergs teurem Sachs.

(The curtain falls.)

VOCABULARY

Separable verbs are indicated by an asterisk.

A

abbiegend, winding, curving.

Abend (-s, -e), *m.*, evening.

abendlich, evening, evening-like.

Abendmahl (-[e]s, -e *or* ⁻er), *n.*, supper.

Abenteuer (-s, -), *m.*, adventure; *also a mode* (*see* Introduction).

Abenteuerer (-s, -), *m.*, adventurer.

Abendtraum (-[e]s, ⁻e), *m.*, evening dream.

aber, but, yet.

abermals, again, once more, anew.

ab*fallen (fiel, a), to fall out, away; drop.

ab*geben (a, e), to deliver.

Abgesang (-[e]s, ⁻e), *m.*, after-song.

Abgeschiedene ∙ Vielfrass (*mode*), secret glutton, gormandizer.

abgewandt, *see* abwenden.

ab*gränzen *or* **ab*grenzen,** to fix the limit; shade.

ab*ringen (a, u), to wrest, obtain.

Absatz (-es, ⁻e), *m.*, end, full close.

ab*schliessen (o, o), to shut off, unlock.

ab*wenden (wandte, gewandt), to turn away, alienate.

ab*ziehen (zog, gezogen), to draw off, withdraw.

ach, ah, oh, ugh.

acht', eighth.

Acht, *f.*, care, attention.

achten, to notice, esteem; *gen.*, take notice of.

ade, farewell.

Ahl' [Ahle] (-, -n), *f.*, awl, punch.

adlig, honored, noble.

Ahn (-en, -en), *m.*, ancestor.

ahnen, to promise, suspect.

ähnlich, like, similar; – **sein,** to be like.

all, all, every, each; – **eins,** all the same.

allein, alone, but, only.

alleinig, only.

allergescheit'st, cleverest of all, most skillful.

allerliebst, most lovely.

allgemein, in common, universal.

Allgewalt (-, -en), *f.*, omnipotence, mighty force.

allmählich *or* **allmälig,** gradually.

allweile, continually, constantly.

allzumal, all at once, all together.

als, as, than, when.

alt, old, ancient; **bei alten,** in olden times (**125**, 23).

ältest' [alt], oldest.

am = an dem.

Amme (-, -n), *f.*, nurse.

Amt (-[e]s, ⁻er), *n.*, office, function.

135

an, at, to the side of, by, for, in, near, on.

an*blasen (ie, a), to breathe upon, excite, inspire; **anblusen,** *vulg.*

an*bringen (brachte, gebracht), to attach, place.

Andenken (-s, –), *n.,* remembrance, souvenir.

ander, other, different, another.

ändern, to change, alter.

anderswo, somewhere else, elsewhere.

an*fallen (fiel, a), to attack, fall to.

Anfang (-[e]s, ″e), *m.,* beginning.

an*fangen (i, a), to begin, commence.

anfänglich, at first, originally.

an*fassen, sich, to join hands.

an*frischen, to renew.

Angabe (–, -n), *f.,* dialogue, statement, declaration.

an*geben (a, e), to give to; **gar auf mein Leben war's angegeben,** really my life was endangered.

an*gehen (ging, gegangen), to concern (57, 16).

an*gehören, to belong to.

angenehm, pleasing, agreeable.

Angst (–, ″e), *f.,* anxiety, fear.

an*halten (ie, a), to pause; **um eine –,** to woo, sue for in marriage.

an*hören, to listen, listen to.

an*kommen (kam, o), to reach, arrive; **wie käm' nun da 'was Gross' drauf an,** who would have thought such dreadful consequences would follow.

an*künden, to announce, give decision.

an*langen, to arrive, assemble.

an*lassen (ie, a), **sich,** to bid fair, do well, commence, take one's turn.

an*merken, to mark down, mark on (a slate).

an*messen (a, e), to make to order, measure (one) for.

an*nehmen (a, genommen), to accept, receive, suppose, assume.

an*richten, to arrange, bring about, start.

ans = an das.

an*sagen, to speak, declare.

an*schauen, to behold, look at, gaze upon.

an*schlafen (ie, a), to acquire by sleep, sleep on.

anschwellend, increasing.

an*sehen (a, e), to observe.

Anstalt (–, -en), *f.,* preparation, disposition, institution.

an*stimmen, to begin (a song), pour forth.

an*streichen (i, i), to stroke, scratch, paint; record (a mistake) (82, 2).

Anstrengung (–, -en), *f.,* effort, strain.

Antrag (-[e]s, ″e), *m.,* matter, communication, proposal.

antworten, to answer, reply.

Äquivoca, *or* **Aequivoca,** words of double meaning.

Arbeit (–, -en), *f.,* work, labor.

arbeiten, to work.

arg, bad, angry, terrible.

ärgerlich, angry, vexed.

ärgern, to vex, enrage.

Ärgernuss *or* **Ärgernis** (-ses, -se), *n.,* vexation, trial.

Arm (-[e]s, -e), *m.,* arm,

arm, poor.

Arm-Hunger (*mode*), keen hunger.

artig, nice, proper, correctly.

Atem (-s), *m.*, breath.

au! ough!

auch, also, even.

Aue (–, -n), *f.*, green meadow, brook.

auf, on, upon, for, toward, to, about; up!

aufblickend, looking up.

auf*bügeln, to smooth out, iron.

auf*fahren (u, a), to start up.

auf*finden (a, u), to find out, ascertain.

auf*flammen, to flame up, flare up.

auf*geben (a, e), to give up, resign.

Aufgebot (-[e]s, -e), *n.*, problem, task.

auf*gehen (ging, gegangen), to go up, open (of a window), rise (sun).

auf*hängen, to palm off upon.

auf*hören, to listen to; *fig.*, cease, stop, leave off.

auf*krächzen, to rouse up and croak.

auf*merken, to watch, look out.

aufmerksam, attentive.

auf*nehmen (a, genommen), to take up, receive.

auf*passen, to watch out, be on the lookout; **aufgepasst!** look out!

auf*regen, to excite, disturb.

Aufregung (–, -en), *f.*, excitement, perturbation.

auf*rufen (ie, u), to call out, call the roll.

Aufruhr (-[e]s, -e), *m.*, uproar, disturbance.

auf*schlagen (u, a), to throw up, construct.

auf*schreiben (ie, ie), to write out.

auf*schwingen (a, u), **sich**, to work up, attain.

auf*stehen (stand, gestanden), to rise, stand up.

auf*suchen, to look up, seek out.

auf*tragen (u, a), to intrust, charge with, put on.

auf*treten, (a, e), to step on, stand on.

Auftritt (-[e]s, -e), *m.*, step, scene (of a play).

auf*tun (tat, getan), to open, reveal.

auf*wachen, to wake up.

auf*ziehen (zog, gezogen), to draw up, arrive.

Aufzug (-[e]s, "e), *m.*, act (of a play); rise.

auf*zwingen (a, u), to force upon.

Auge (-s, -n), *n.*, eye.

Augenblick (-[e]s, -e), *m.*, moment.

aus, out of, from.

aus*dehnen, to extend.

aus*drücken, to express, utter.

auseinander, apart; let go.

auseinander*fahren (u, a), to separate, go apart.

aus*erküren (o, o), to choose, select.

aus*ersehen (a, e), to choose.

Ausgang (-[e]s, "e), *m.*, door, exit.

aus*halten (ie, a), to hold out, endure, keep it up.

Ausnahme (–, -n), *f.*, exception.

aus*richten, to accomplish, to do.

Ausruf (-[e]s, -e), *m.*, cry, exclamation.

aus*sagen, to say, express.

aus*schauen, to look.

Ausschlag (-[e]s, ˝e), *m.,* first blow, decision, veto.

Ausschlag-Stimme (-, -n), *f.,* veto.

aus*sehen (a, e), to look, appear.

auswendlich, outside.

B

Bäcker (-s, -), *m.,* baker.

Bader (-s, -), *m.,* barber, cupper.

bald, soon, quickly.

bäldlich, soon, quickly.

balgen, to struggle, fight.

ballen, to shake (the fist).

Band (-[e]s, ˝er), *n.,* ribbon, streamer.

bang, timidly, frightened; **einem – sein** *or* **werden,** to be afraid; **'s ward einem bang,** 't was frightful.

Bank (-, ˝e), *f.,* bench.

bannen, to conjure, honor.

Bar (-s), *n. and m.,* stave, bar; a definite portion of a master-song.

Bart (-[e]s, ˝e), *m.,* beard.

bauen, to build, construct.

Baum (-[e]s, ˝e), *m.,* tree, gallows.

beachten, to pay attention, mind.

beben, to throb, vibrate.

bedecken, to cover.

bedenken (bedachte, bedacht), to consider, ponder ; **hat man je so einen Feind bedacht?** does one treat a foe like that ?

bedenklich, doubtful.

bedeuten, to mean, signify.

bedeutungsvoll, significant, meaning.

Beding (-[e]s, -e), *m.,* condition, stipulation.

Bedingung (-, -en), *f.,* condition, stipulation.

bedrängen, to oppress, crowd, abuse.

bedürftig, needy, troubled.

beerben, to inherit, be heir to.

befehlen (a, o), to command; bless; commend (to).

befreien, to set free, free (from).

begehen (beging, begangen), to solemnize, celebrate; perpetrate.

begehren, to aspire, desire; **die Freiung –,** to teach the particulars.

begehrlich, desirous, envious.

begeistern, to inspire.

Begeistern (-s), *n.,* inspiration.

Begeisterung (-, -en), *f.,* inspiration; enthusiasm.

beginnen (a, o), to begin, commence.

begleiten, to escort, accompany.

begraben (u, a), to bury; buried.

begreifen (begriff, begriffen), to comprehend, understand.

begrenzen, to border (on).

Begriff (-[e]s, -e), *m.,* idea; **im –,** on the point of.

begrüssen, to greet, bow.

behagen, to please, make happy.

behalten (ie, a), to retain, keep, remember.

behangen (i, a), to be hung with, be laden.

behüten, to forefend, forbid, protect.

bei, by, with, at the house of, while at, on one's person; **– Zeit,** early.

beide, both, the two.

beifällig, approving.

bei*kommen (kam, o), **sich – lassen,** to dare, presume.

beim = bei dem.

beisammen, together.

Beispiel (-[e]s, -e), *n.*, example, illustration.

bei*stehen (stand, gestanden), to stand by, support, agree.

bei*stimmen, to agree, consent.

Bekämpfung (–, -en), *f.*, combat, (the) contending against.

bekommen (bekam, o), to get, receive; agree with; prosper, thrive.

belagern, to besiege.

belegen, to cover; *fig.*, to prove.

Beleuchtung (–, -en), *f.*, illumination.

belieben, to be agreeable, like; choose.

bemächtigen, to seize, master.

bemeistern, to master, control.

beobachten, to observe, behold.

bequem, convenient, at ease, comfortable.

beraten (ie, a), to take counsel.

bereit, ready.

bereiten, to prepare, make ready.

bereits, already.

Berg (-[e]s, -e), *m.*, mountain.

bergen (a, o), to conceal, shelter; **geborgen,** safe, cared for.

Bericht (-[e]s, -e), *m.*, information, report.

berichten, to complete; report completely.

besänftigend, soothingly.

beschäftigt, busied, occupied.

bescheiden, modest.

bescheiden (ie, ie), to award, grant; **beschieden,** fallen to one's lot, assigned, awarded.

bescheinen (ie, ie), to appear, shine upon.

bescheren, to bestow upon; **beschert,** presented.

beschiessen (o, o), to fire upon; **. . ., hier nichts beschiesst,** is not the point.

beschliessen (o, o), to determine, decree.

beschuhen, to shoe; **unbeschuht,** unshod.

Beschwer, *f. and n.*, pain.

Beschwerde (–, -n), *f.*, sorrow, fatigue, trouble, difficulty, quarrel.

beschweren, to annoy, burden, charge.

beschwerlich, in trouble, painful.

beschwören (o, o), to implore, conjure, beseech.

besehen (a, e), to inspect, look at.

besiegen, to overcome, win.

besinnen (a, o), to reflect, meditate.

besonder, particular, especial.

besonders, especially.

besser, *from* **gut,** better.

Besserung (–, -en), *f.*, recovery, improvement.

besessen, possessed, intoxicated.

besiegen, to overcome, conquer.

besinnen (a, o), to reflect.

Besinnen (-s), *n.*, wits.

best, am -en, best.

bestehen (bestand *or* bestund, bestanden), to stand an examination; be getting along; woo; insist; defend (129, 23); consist of, undertake, stand.

bestellen, to order, appoint, arrange.

bestimmt, appointed, determined upon, fixed, definite.

Besuch (-[e]s, -e), *m.*, visit, call.

betäuben, to stupefy.

Beteuerung (-, -en), *f.*, passion, endearment.

betören, to mock, make a fool of.

betrachten, to regard, observe.

betreffen (betraf, o), to befall, meet with; **was ... betrifft,** concerning, as for the ...

betreten (a, e), to enter, see.

Betretenheit (-, -en), *f.*, consternation.

betrüben, to sadden.

Bett (-[e]s, -en), *n.*, bed.

bewaffnen, to arm.

bewahren, to keep, preserve, guard from, contain.

bewegen, to move.

Bewegung (-, -en), *f.*, action, movement.

beweinen, to rue, lament, regret.

beweisen (ie, ie), to prove, show.

bewenden (bewandte, bewandt), arranged, decreed.

bewies, *see* **beweisen.**

bezaubern, to enchant.

bezwingen (a, u), to control, subdue.

biblisch, biblical, from the Bible.

bieder, honest, upright.

Biederkeit (-, -en), *f.*, honesty, sincerity.

biegen (o, o), to bend, bow.

bieten (o, o), to offer, give; afford.

Bild (-[e]s, -er), *n.*, picture, portrait.

bilden, to form, fashion, shape.

Bildnis (-ses, -se), *n.*, image, likeness.

billig, fairly, reasonable.

binden (a, u), to bind.

birg, *see* **bergen.**

bis, until, till, as far as.

bist, *see* **sein.**

bitten (a, e), to entreat, ask.

Bitte (-, n), *f.*, entreaty.

bitter, bitter, sharp, severe, badly.

blasen (ie, a), to blow.

Blatt (-[e]s, "er), *n.*, leaf, sheet, manuscript.

blau, blue; *also a tone.*

Blau - Rittersporn (*mode*), blue knight-spur.

bleiben (ie, ie), to remain, stay; be.

bleich, pale, white.

Bleisaft (-[e]s, "e), *m.*, lead-juice.

Blick (-[e]s, -e), *m.*, look, glance, sight, manner; vision (105, 17).

blicken, to look, gaze.

blind, blind, clouded; **-e Meinung,** obscure meaning.

blinken (blinkern), to gleam, glitter.

bloss, bare, naked; only, simply, first.

Blüh und Wachs (*mode*), bloom and growth.

Blum (*tech.*), ornaments, embellishments.

Blume (-, -n), *f.*, flower.

Blumenhag (-[e]s, -e), *m.*, flower inclosure, garden, hay-field.

Blumenkränzlein (-s, -), *n.*, wreath of flowers.

Blumenstock (-[e]s, "e), *m.*, flower-stick, flower-pot.

Blut (-[e]s), *n.*, blood.

Blüte (-, -n), *f.*, blossom, bloom.

Bock (-[e]s, "e), *m.*, goat, buck, ram.

Bockfell (-[e]s, -e), *n.*, goatskin.

Boden (-s, " *or* -), *m.*, floor, ground.

böse, angry, naughty.

boshaft, malicious.

Bosheit (-, -en), *f.*, **malice.**

bot, *see* **bieten.**

Brauch (-[e]s, ″e), *m.*, custom, usage.

brauchen, to need.

Braut (-, ″e), *f.*, bride, betrothed.

Brautführer (-s, -), *m.*, best man.

Bräutigam (-s, -e), *m.*, betrothed, bridegroom.

brechen (a, o), to break, transgress; disappear (105, 17).

breit, broad, wide.

brennen (brannte, gebrannt), to burn.

Brettbodengerüst[e] (-es, -e), *n.*, platform of boards, stage.

Brief (-[e]s, -e), *m.*, letter.

bringen (brachte, gebracht), to bring; accomplish.

Brot (-[e]s, -e), *n.*, bread.

Bruch (-[e]s, ″e), *m.*, break, cleavage.

brummen, to grumble.

Brunst (-, ″e), *f.*, fervor, ardor.

brünstig, ardently.

Brust (-, ″e), *f.*, breast.

Brusttuch (-[e]s, ″er), *n.*, kerchief.

brütend, brooding.

Bube (-n, -n), *m.*, boy, apprentice, lad.

Buch (-[e]s, ″er), *n.*, book.

Buckel (-s, -), *m.*, hump, bunch, *vulg.*, back; **da hieb ich dem den - voll,** I just gave him a good drubbing.

bücken, to bow, bend.

Bügel (-s, -), *m.*, flatiron, tailor's goose.

Buhle (-n, -n), *m. and f.*, lover, mistress, love.

Bühne (-, -n), *f.*, scaffold, stage (of a theater).

bunt, gay, surprising.

Burg (-, -en), *f.*, castle, stronghold, village.

Bürge (-n, -n), *m.*, bail, security.

Bürger (-s,-), *m.*, citizen, inhabitant.

Bursche (-n, -n), *m.*, fellow, apprentice.

Busen (-s, -), *m.*, bosom, breast.

büssen, to suffer; **für etwas -,** to pay for, satisfy, indulge.

Buttglänzende (*mode*), rosy-gleaming-thread.

C

carieren, to go hungry.

Chor (-[e]s, ″e), *m.*, chorus, choir.

Chor (-[e]s, ″e), *n.*, choir loft, choir (of a church).

Choral (-[e]s, ″e), *m.*, choral, choral song.

Christ (-es), *m.*, Christ.

Chronik (-, -en), *f.*, chronicle, record.

D

da, since, when, there, here, present, at that time.

dabei, by it, present, with it, at the same time.

dabei*halten (ie, a), to stand by, to be ready.

daheim, at home, in doors; **liess ich ihn gern -,** might he indulge in at home.

dahin, thither, that far, to it.

dahinter, behind it, to it, in it.

damit, therewith, in order that, with it, that those, etc.

dämmern, to grow dusky, be twilight.

dämpfen, to muffle, modulate.

danach, *see* **darnach.**

daneben, besides, along with it.

Dank (-[e]s), *m.*, thanks, acknowledgement.

danken, to thank.

dankenswert, worthy of thanks.

dann, then.

dannen, thence (**von** –).

daran, thereon, thereat, at it; **sonst denkt ihr mir** –! do you think I am to be joked with!

daran*denken (dachte, gedacht), to ponder, think over, think of.

d[a]ran*kommen (kam, o), to be involved; **kommt der auch daran,** does it pinch there, too?

d[a]rauf, thereon, thereupon, thereafter; – **zu,** at him, here goes; **drauf und zu,** up and at; **drauf und dran,** join the fight.

d[a]rauf*hören, to give heed, heed.

d[a]rauf*schlagen (u, a), to take a hand, join in the fight.

daraus, out of it, from it; – **nicht klug werden,** to make nothing out of it.

dar*bieten (o, o), **sich,** to present itself.

darein, in it, into which, in which.

d[a]rein*geben (a, e), to give into the bargain, throw in.

d[a]rein*schlagen (u, a), to take a hand, fall to and strike a blow.

darin [d'rin], in that, therein, in this matter.

darnach, accordingly; **das mag denn wohl auch** – **sein,** I presume that that is the kind of singer he is.

darob [drob], on that account, therefore.

darüber, about it, over it, concerning that, of that, on account of that.

darum [drum], therefore, on that account, for that reason.

darf, *see* **dürfen.**

dar*stellen, to exhibit.

dass, that, if, so that; – **nicht,** lest.

dauern, to last, continue.

davon, therefrom, of that, from that, away, off.

dazu, thereto, besides, for it, for the purpose, at the same time.

dazu*kommen (kam, o), to add to it; *fig.*, bring news (68, 13); come by (a thing).

dein, thy, thine, you, yours.

demütig, humbly, submissive.

denken (dachte, gedacht), to think.

Denkmünze (–, -n), *f.*, medal.

denn, then, for.

der, the, this, that, he, who, which.

derb, steady, rough, coarse.

deren, of them, of whom.

derlei, that sort, such music (116, 13).

derweile, in the meantime.

dess' [dessen], whose.

deuten, to indicate, be a token, augur, hint.

deutsch, German.

Deutung (–, -en), *f.*, meaning.

dich, thee, you.

dicht, close, tight, thick, coarse (64, 13).

Dichte [Dichtheit], *f.*, versifying, poetry.

dichten, to compose poetry.

Dichter (-s, –), *m.*, poet.

Dichter-Reck' (-en, -en), *m.*, hero poet.

Dichterei (-, -en), *f.*, poetry, bad
poetry.

dichterisch, poetic.

Dichterpreis (-es, -e), *m.*, title *or*
name of poet.

Dichtertraum (-[e]s, ⁻e), *m.*, poet's
dream.

Dichtkunst (-, ⁻e), *f.*, composition
(of poetry).

dickstämmig, sturdy, large-trunked.

dictieren, to dictate.

Dieb (-[e]s, -e), *m.*, thief.

Differenz (-, -en), *f.*, alteration,
change.

Ding (-[e]s, -e *or* -er), *n.*, matter,
affair; **vor allen -en,** above all
things, first and foremost.

Dinte [Tinte] (-, -n), *f.*, ink.

doch, yet, however, nevertheless,
but, at least, then.

Dohle (-, -n), *f.*, jay, rook.

Dorn (-[e]s, ⁻er *or* -en), *m.*, thorn.

Dornenhecke (-, -n), *f.*, thorn hedge.

dort, there, yonder; **wie – so hier,**
in every particular.

dorthin, that way, thither.

Draht (-[e]s, -e *or* ⁻e), *m.*, thread,
wire.

Drang (-[e]s), *m.*, pressure, stress.

dran, *see* daran.

drängen, to hurry, press; **gedrängt,**
crowded.

drauf, *see* darauf.

draus, *see* daraus.

drei, three.

drein, *see* darein.

drein*schlagen, *see* darein*schla·
gen.

dreist, bold, with assurance.

dreschen (a *or* o, o), to thrash,
cudgel.

drin, *see* darin.

dringen (a, u), to press, insist, im-
portune; **wird erst auf die Feh·
lerprobe gedrungen?** shall we
count his mistakes first? (51, 1).

dritte, third.

drohen, to threaten.

drohend, threatening(ly).

drüben [darüben], yonder, on that
side.

drücken, to press, restrain.

drum, *see* darum.

du, thou, you.

Duft (-es, ⁻e), *m.*, fragrance, scent.

duften, to be fragrant.

duftig, fragrant.

dumm, stupid, foolish.

Dummheit (-, -en), *f.*, folly, stup-
idity.

Dummrian (-s, -e), *m.*, stupid fellow.

dünken, sich, to imagine one's self;
appear, fancy; **was der sich
dünkt?** what airs he puts on!

dünn, thin.

Dunst (-es, ⁻e), *m.*, vapor; – ma·
chen, to cast a mist before the
eyes.

durch, through, by, through the
instrumentality of.

durchhallen, *also sep.*, to resound,
ring.

durchklingen, *also sep.*, (a, u), to
resound.

durchscheinen (ie, ie), to light up,
illuminate.

durch*schlagen (u, a), to force
through; **sich –,** to cut (one's)
way through.

dürfen (durfte, gedurft), to be per-
mitted, be allowed, need, dare,
have reason, may, can.

dürr, arid, dry, withered.

dursten, to be thirsty.

E

eben, even, just, exactly, precisely.

ebenbürtig, of equal birth.

ebenfalls, likewise.

echt, genuine, unalterated, pure.

Ecke (-, -n), *f.*, corner.

Eckhäuser, *pl., n.*, corner houses.

edel [edle], noble.

eh', ehe, ere, before.

Ehe (-, -n), *f.*, wedlock, matrimony, marriage.

eher, sooner, earlier, rather.

Ehestand (-[e]s), *m.*, wedlock, matrimony.

Ehgemahl (-[e]s, -e). *n.*, wife.

ehlich, matrimonial, wedded.

Ehre (-, -n), *f.*, honor.

ehren, to honor, revere.

Ehrenmänner, *pl., m.*, men of honor.

ehrerbietig, reverential, respectful.

ehrlich, honorably, nobly, in wedlock.

ei, why! hey! ay!

Eidam (-[e]s, -e), *m.*, son-in-law.

Eifer (-s), *m.*, zeal, wrath, flutter.

eiferlich, jealous.

Eifersucht, *f.*, jealousy.

eifrigst, jealous, industrious.

eigen, own, peculiar to, gifted, singular, strange.

Eigen (-s), *n.*, property.

eilen, to hasten; **geeilt,** fast, rapidly.

eilig, quickly, hastily.

ein, a, an, one; *fig.*, some, any.

ein, in.

einander, each other.

einbrechend, approaching.

einerlei, alike, of one sort.

einfach, simple, plain.

Einfall (-[e]s, *"*e), *m.*, idea.

ein*fallen (fiel, a), to occur to one, think of.

einfältig, simple.

ein*fassen, to encompass, inclose, compose.

ein*finden (a, u), **sich,** to appear, be present.

ein*führen, to lead in, introduce, make (one) acquainted, teach.

ein*gehen (ging, gegangen), to enter, go in.

Eingang (-[e]s, *"*e), *m.*, entrance.

ein*geben (a, e), to reveal, give in.

ein*greifen (i, i), to take from, plagiarize.

ein*halten (ie, a), to hold in, hush; **haltet ein,** hold on.

ein*henken, to lean, cling.

ein*nähen, to sew in, dress.

einig, only, solely, united, harmoniously.

ein*kehren, to attain, turn in.

ein*laden (u, a), to invite.

Einladung (-, -en), *f.*, invitation.

ein*lassen (ie, a), to let in, admit.

Einleitung (-, -en), *f.*, arrangement, disposition.

einmal, once, one time; **nicht** -, not even.

einmal, once upon a time, one day, some day.

ein*richten, to arrange, dispose.

ein*schliessen (o, o), to inclose, admit, receive (into).

ein*schneien, to snow in; **einge-schneit,** snow-bound.

ein*schreiben (ie, ie), to register.

einst, once.

ein*stecken, to pocket, put in the pocket.

ein*tauschen, to convert, transmute.

ein*treten (a, e), to enter, step in, begin.

einzig, single, solitary, unique, one

eitel, vain, useless. [single.

Eitel - Brot - und - Wasser (*mode*), nothing but bread und water.

Eitelkeit, *f.*, vanity, foolishness.

Elster (–, -n), *f.*, magpie, jay.

Eltern, *pl.*, parents.

empfangen (i, a), to receive.

empfehlen (a, o), to recommend.

Emsigkeit, *f.*, activity, diligence, earnestness.

Ende (-s, -n), *n.*, end; **am –,** after all, perhaps.

endlich, at last, finally.

endlos, endless, without end.

eng, narrow, tight, close.

Engel (-s, –), *m.*, angel.

Englische-Zinn (*mode*), English-tin.

entbieten (o, o), to announce, bid, summon.

entfernen, to remove, leave off.

Entfernung (–, -en), *f.*, distance, removal, remoteness.

Entführung (–, -en), *f.*, abduction, elopement.

entgegen, against, toward.

enthalten (ie, a), to hold, contain.

entladen (u, a), to get rid of.

entlang, alongside of, against, along.

entnehmen (a, entnommen), to take away; *fig.*, understand, hear.

entragend, towering above, projecting over.

entrinnen (a, o), to depart, escape.

entschlagen (u, a), to break away from, leave off.

entsprechen (a, o), to correspond to, agree with, suit.

entstehen (entstand, entstanden), to arise from, ensue.

entstellen, to distort, deform; **entstellt,** sung it wrong (129, 15).

entwachsen (u, a), to grow from, supply.

entwandt, *see* **entwenden.**

entweichen (i, i), to run away, fear.

entwenden (entwandte, entwandt), to steal, lift.

entwickeln, to develop.

entzweien, to separate.

er, he, it.

erbarmen, to have pity, take pity.

Erbe (-s), *n.*, wealth, inheritance.

erblühen, to blossom out, bloom.

Erde (–, -n), *f.*, earth.

erdacht, *see* **erdenken.**

erdenken (erdachte, erdacht), to conceive.

erdreisten, sich, to aspire, be bold.

Erdreistung, *f.*, offense, insolence, boldness.

erfahren (u, a), to learn, attain, experience.

erfinden (a, u), to find out, invent, compose.

Erfrischung (–, -en), *f.*, refreshment.

Erfüllung, *f.*, fulfillment.

ergehen (erging, ergangen), to happen, come out, come to pass, stand.

ergiessen (o, o), to pour out.

erglühen, to glow, burn.

Ergriffenheit, *f.*, emotion

erheben (o, o), to rise up, get up.

erhöhen, to raise, elevate.

erhören, to be heard of, hear.

erkennen (erkannte, erkannt), to recognize, disclose.

erkiest, *see* **erküren.**

erklären, to explain, declare, decree.

erklingen (a, u), to ring out.

erkoren, *see* **erküren.**

erkühnen, sich, to dare, venture.

erküren [erkiesen] (erkor, erkoren), to choose, elect; **wär' keinem sie erkoren,** though chosen by none.

erlauben, to allow, permit.

erlauschen, to hear.

erleben, to experience, live (a thing).

erlösen, to deliver, release.

ermutigend, encouraging.

ernennen (ernannte, ernannt), to name, appoint.

erneuern, to renew, revive; **sich –,** be renewed.

ernst, serious, staid.

Ernst (-es), *m.*, seriousness.

ernstlich, serious, really.

erreichen, to reach, attain, master.

erringen (a, u), to obtain by effort, attain after a struggle.

erschauen, to behold, see.

erscheinen (ie, ie), to appear, dawn.

erschliessen (o, o), to reveal, disclose.

erschrecken, to frighten.

erschrecken (erschrak, o), to be terrified.

erschrickt, frightened.

erschwingen (a, u), to win, achieve.

ersehen (a, e), to perceive, see.

ersehnen, to long for, yearn.

ersingen (a, u), to win by singing.

ersinnen (a, o), to think out, dream of, become conscious.

erst, first, scarcely.

erstreiten (erstritt, erstritten), to win out.

erteilen, to impart, award.

ertosen, to rumble over; *fig.*, exult.

erträglich, endurably, tolerable.

erwachen, to awake, arouse.

erwachsen (u, a), to arise, happen (to one).

erwägen (o, o), to weigh, ponder, learn, consider.

erwählen, to elect, choose.

erwarten, to await, expect, wait for.

erwecken, to awaken.

erweichen (i, i), to give away, run away; fear, yield.

erwerben (a, o), to win, obtain, woo.

erwidern, to reply, answer.

erzählen, to narrate, tell.

erzeigen, to experience, find.

es, it; *before a verb,* there.

Esel (-s, –), *m.*, donkey.

Eseltreiber (-s, –), *m.*, donkey-driver, boor.

etliche, some, several.

etwa, possibly, about.

euch, to you, you.

euer, your, yours, of you.

Eule (–, -n), *f.*, owl.

ewig, eternal, immortal.

F

Faden (-s, ⁔), *m.*, thread.

Fall (-[e]s, ⁔e), *m.*, case, instance.

Falle (-, -n), *f.*, trap, snare.

fallen (fiel, a), to fall.

falsch, wrong, out of tune, away; -er **Atem**, faulty breathing.

Falsch-Geband, faulty versification.

Farbetunke (-, -n), *f.*, dyer's pit.

fassen, to grasp, clasp, gage, sew, catch; **sich gefasst machen**, prepare one's self; **gefasst**, rest assured.

fast, almost.

faul, rotten, corrupt; **doch steht's drum** -, nevertheless it's all wrong.

Faust (-, ⁔e), *f.*, fist.

Feder (-, -n), *f.*, feather, pen.

fehl, faulty, wrong: **der Junker ist – am Ort**, has not had orthodox instructions.

fehlen, to be lacking, not present, be wrong; **das fehlte auch noch**, that would be the last straw.

Fehler (-s, -), *m.*, mistake, fault.

Fehlerprobe (-, -n), *f.*, examination of faults (made by a candidate).

fehlervoll, faultily, full of faults.

feiern, to celebrate.

fein, fine, refined, cute; – **sacht**, very fine.

Feind (-[e]s -e), *m.*, enemy, foe.

Fell (-[e]s, -e), *n.*, skin, hide.

Fengel (*mode*), fennel.

Fenster (-s, -), *n.*, window.

fern, far, distant.

Ferne (-, -n), *f.*, distance.

Ferse (-, -n), *f.*, heel, foot.

fertig, through, done, finished.

Fest (-[e]s, -e), *n.*, festival, feast.

fest, firm, exactly.

festlich, solemn, festive.

festgebannt, spell-bound.

Festgewand (-[e]s, ⁔er *or* -e), *n.*, holiday dress.

Feuer (s, -), *n.*, fire.

feurig, fervent, ardently.

finden (a, u), to find; **sich** –, to offer one's self (108, 6).

Findung (-, -en), *f.*, invention.

Fink (-en, -en), *m.*, finch.

finster, gloomy, dark.

Flause (-, -n), *f.*, juggling, false pretense, humbug, fooling.

flechten (o, o), to braid, weave.

Fleck (-[e]s, -e), *m.*, spot, place.

flecken, to put on heel pieces, heel, tap.

Fleisch (-[e]s), *n.*, flesh.

Fleiss (-[e]s), *m.*, industry, diligence.

fleissig, industrious, busy.

flicken, to sew.

Flickgesang (-[e]s, ⁔e), *m.*, patchwork-song.

Flieder (-s, -), *m.*, elder tree.

fliehen (o, o), to flee, fly.

fliessen (o, o), to flow.

Fluch (-[e]s, ⁔e), *m.*, curse, ban.

Flucht, *f.*, flight, escape, rout.

flüchtig, flying, flighty, quickly.

Flug (-[e], ⁔e), *m.*, brood, flock, flight.

Flügel (-s, -), *m.*, wings, pinions.

Flügelpaar (-[e]s, -e), *n.*, pinions.

Flur (-, -en), *f.*, floor, fields.

Fluss (-es, ⁔e), *m.*, river.

folgen, to follow, *dat.*

folgsam, obedient, well-taught.

Foliant (-en, -en), *m.*, folio, volume.

fördern, to promote, assist.

forschend, searching, inquiringly.

fort, away, gone, off.

fortan, henceforth.

fort*fahren (u, a), to continue, resume.

fort*lassen (ie, a), to let away, let alone.

fort*laufen (ie, au), to run away.

fort*scheren (o, o), **sich,** to go away, make (yourself) scarce.

fort*singen (a, u), to keep on singing.

fortwährend, continually.

Frage (-, -n), *f.,* question.

fragen, to ask, question.

Franken, *n.,* Franconia.

Frau (-, -en), *f.,* woman, wife.

Fräulein (-s, -), *n.,* miss, young lady.

frech, insolent, impudent.

frei, freely, frankly.

freien, to woo, marry; **gefreit,** wooed.

Freier (-s, -), *m.,* suitor; -**füssen,** suitor's footing.

Frei-Gesang (-[e]s, "e), *m.,* mastersong.

Freiheit (-, -en), *f.,* freedom.

Freiung (-, -en), *f.,* trial.

fremd, strange, foreign, unknown, not one's own.

freuen, sich, to be glad, rejoice, take pleasure (in).

Freund (-[e]s, -e), *m.,* friend.

Freundin (-, -nen), *f.,* friend.

freundlich, kind, familiar.

friedsam, peaceful.

frisch, fresh, jovial.

Frisch-Pomeranzen (*mode*), fresh orange.

froh, glad, happy.

Frösch (*tone*), frog.

Frost (-[e]s, "e), *m.,* frost, chill.

Frucht (-, "e), *f.,* fruit, crops.

früh, early.

fügen, to join, unite.

fühlen, to feel.

führen, to lead, guide; **zu Gemüte** -, let me impress it upon you.

fünfzig, fifty.

für, for, in behalf of, in return for; **was** -, what sort of . . .

fürchten, to fear, be afraid.

furchtsam, fearful, in fear.

Fürst (-en, -en), *m.,* prince.

fürwahr, in truth.

Fuss (-es, "e), *m.,* foot; **auf die** "e, start along.

Füsschen (-s, -), *n.,* little feet, tootsies, footlets.

Fusstritt (-[e]s, -e), *m.,* kick.

füttern, to feed.

G

Gabe (-, -n), *f.,* gift, prize.

Galgen (-s, -), *m.,* gallows.

Galle (-, -n), *f.,* gall, bile, anger.

gallicht, *see* **gallig.**

gallig, spleeny, rancorous.

ganz, quite, whole, entirely.

gar, quite, even, at all.

garstig, nasty, dirty.

Garten (-s, "), *m.,* garden.

Gasse (-, -n), *f.,* street, lane, alley.

Gassenhauer (-s, -), *m.,* street songs, country ballads.

Gast (-[e]s, "e), *m.,* guest, visitor.

Geband (-[e]s, "e) = **Gebinde,** *n.,* verse, measure.

Gebärde (–, -n), *f.*, glance, countenance.

gebären (a, o), to bring forth, be born.

geben (a, e), to give; **es gibt**, there is; **verloren** –, give up, withdraw.

geboren, *see* **gebären.**

Gebot (-[e]s, -e), *n.*, sign, token, symbol, command, commandment; call, summons (66, 18).

Gebrauch (-[e]s, "e), *m.*, use, custom.

Gebüsch (-[e]s, -e), *n.*, shrubbery, thicket.

Gedanke (-n, -n), *m.*, thought, idea.

gedankenvoll, plunged in deep thought.

gedenken (dachte, gedacht), to recall, remember.

gedeihen (ie, ie), to prosper, assist.

Gedicht (-[e]s, -e), *n.*, poem.

Gedränge (-s), *n.*, throng, crowd.

Geduld, *f.*, patience.

Gefahr (–, -en), *f.*, danger.

gefährlich, dangerous.

gefallen (gefiel, a), to please, be one's pleasure.

Geflunker (-s), *n.*, boasting, display.

Gefieder (-s), *n.*, plumage, feathers.

Gefühl (-[e]s, -e), *n.*, feeling.

gegen, toward, against, near.

gegenüber, opposite.

geheim, in secret, secretly.

gehen (ging, gegangen), to walk, go; **'s mag – oder stehen,** do what we will; **spazieren** –, to take a walk.

gehören, to belong to.

geigen, to play the fiddle, serenade.

Geist (-[e]s, -er), *m.*, spirit.

geistesabwesend, absent-minded, rapt.

Geistesentrücktheit, *f.*, trance.

geizen, to be parsimonious; **– nach,** to aspire to.

Gekreisch (-[e]s, -e), *n.*, **Schmerz-,** cry of pain.

Gekreisse (-s), *n.*, muddle, mixture.

Gelächter (-s), *n.*, laughter.

gelangen . . . lassen, to have directed (einem).

Gelblöwenhaut (*mode*), yellow-lion-skin.

Gelbveiglein (*mode*), yellow violet.

Geld (-[e]s, -er), *n.*, money.

gelegen, to be situated, convenient; **– sein (an einem Dinge),** be of consequence, *or* of importance.

Geleise (-s, –), *n.*, track, series, rut.

geleiten, to escort, accompany.

Geliebte (-n, -n), *m.*, lover.

Geliebte (-n, -n), *f.*, mistress, sweetheart.

Gemeinde (–, -n), *f.*, congregation,

gelingen (a, u), *impersonal,* **(einem),** to succeed, prosper, speed.

geloben, to promise, vow.

gelten (a, o), to be worth, award, pay, concern, be considered, be adjudged, be a case for (119, 6); be necessary (120, 13).

Gemahl (-[e]s, -e), *m.*, husband, consort.

Gemäss (-es, -e), *n.*, measure (of music). people.

Gemeine (-n, -n), *m.*, common people, the poor; *adj.*, common.

Gemenge (-s), *n.*, crowd, host, medley.

Gemerk (-[e]s, -e), *n.*, tribunal, platform enclosed by curtains for the "marker" (see Introduction).

Gemüt (-[e]s, -er), *n.*, mind, heart, disposition, nature.

gen, *prep. obs. and poetical for* **gegen**.

genannt, *see* **nennen**.

genau, exactly, particular.

Genoss (-en, -en), *m.*, companion, colleague.

genug, enough, sufficient.

Genüge, *f.*, pledge enough, sufficiency.

genügen, to suffice, satisfy, be satisfied.

gerade, straight, upright, exactly; **gerad' aus**, straightway, straight ahead.

geraten (ie, a), to hit upon, produce, be successful with.

Geräusch (-[e]s, -e), *n.*, rustle, noise.

gerben, to tan (a hide); *fig.*, thrash, lick.

Gerber (-s, -), *m.*, tanner.

gereichen, to turn to, prove, redound to (one's honor).

gereuen, **sich**, to repent.

Gericht (-[e]s, -e), *n.*, trial, tribunal.

gering, common, trifling, small.

gern, gladly, willingly.

Gerstenstang (-, -en), *f.*, barleystick.

Gesang (-[e]s, "e), *m.*, song, art of singing.

Gesätz (-es, -e), *n.*, part, stanza, section.

Geschäft (-[e]s, -e), *n.*, business.

geschehen (a, e), to happen, take place.

gescheit, wise, skillful; **nicht recht** –, foolish (117, 12).

Geschichte (-, -n), *f.*, tale, affair, history.

Geschlamb' (-s), *n.*, mess, slop.

Geschlumbfer (-s), *n.*, slovenliness; **da gibt's Geschlamb' und** –, and there's a mess and a mixture.

Geschrei (-[e]s), *n.*, cry, bawling.

geschwind, quickly, rapid.

gesegnen, to bless.

Gesell (-en, -en), *m.*, journeyman, fellow, comrade, pupil.

Gesetz (-es, -e), *n.*, law, regulation.

Gesicht (-[e]s, -e), *n.*, face, countenance.

gespannt, attentive, intent.

Gespenst (-[e]s, -er), *n.*, ghost, specter.

Gespött (-[e]s, -e), *n.*, mocking, jibes.

Gespräch (-[e]s, -e), *n.*, talk, discourse.

gestatten, to permit, allow.

gestehen (gestand, gestanden), to admit, confess, state.

gestern, yesterday.

Gesträuch (-[e]s, -e), *n.*, shrubbery, bushes.

Gesumm' (-s), *n.*, humming.

Getön (-[e]s), *n.*, sound, music, tones.

Getränk (-[e]s, -e), *n.*, drink.

getrauen, to intrust, confide; compete (125, 16).

getraut, engaged, betrothed.

getreulich, faithfully.

getrost, comfortable, peaceful(ly).

Gevatter (-s, -n), *m.*, godfather, sponsor.

Gevatterin (-, -nen), *f.*, god mother.

gewännet, *see* **gewinnen.**

Gewähr, *f.*, proof, guaranty.

gewahren, to become aware of, perceive.

gewähren, to grant, fulfill, vouch.

Gewalt (-, -en), *f.*, power.

gewaltsam, by force.

Gewerk (-[e]s, -e), *n.*, works, manufactures.

Gewicht (-[e]s, -e), *n.*, weight, importance.

gewiegt, cradled, moving, rocked.

gewill[e]t, willing, agreed.

gewinnen (a, o), to win.

Gewinnst [Gewunst] (-[e]s, -e), *m.*, winning, profit.

Gewirr[e] (-s), *n.*, complication, confusion.

gewiss, certain, sure.

Gewissen (-s), *n.*, conscience.

gewisslich, certainly.

gewitzigt [gewitzt], taught wisdom.

Gewohnheit (-, -en), *f.*, habit, custom.

gewohnt, accustomed.

gewonnen, *see* **gewinnen.**

giessen (o, o), to pour.

Gilde (-, -n), *f.*, guild.

Glanz (-es), *m.*, flash of light, splendor.

glänzend, gleaming.

Glasskugel (-, -n), *f.*, water globe, glass globe.

glatt, smooth.

glauben, mir, to believe.

gleich, like; *adv.*, immediately.

gleiten (glitt, geglitten), to glide, slide.

Glied (-[e]s, -er). *n.*, member, limb.

Glocke (-, -n), *f.*, bell.

Glockenhall (-[e]s, -e), *m.*, chime of bells. sound of bells.

Glück (-[e]s), *n.*, luck, happiness, good fortune; – **auf,** good luck.

glücken, to succeed, prosper.

glücklich, happily, fortunate.

glückwünschend, congratulating.

glühend, glowing.

Glühwurm (-[e]s, "er), *m.*, glow-worm, firefly.

Glut (-, -en), *f.*, fervor, glow, heat.

Gnade (-. -n) *f.*, favor, graciousness.

Gold (-[e]s), *n.*, gold.

golden, gold, golden.

Goldschmied (-[e]s, -e), *m.*, goldsmith.

Goliath (-s), *m.*, Goliath (a giant).

gönnen, to grant, give, not to grudge, owe.

Gott (-[e]s, "er), *m.*, God.

Gottesdienst (-[e]s, -e), *m.*, church service.

Grab (-[e]s, "er), *n.*, grave, death.

grad', exactly; – **hin,** all at once.

Gram (-[e]s), *m.*, hatred, aversion, grief.

grämen, to be vexed, grieve.

grauen, to dread, fear.

greifen (griff, gegriffen), to seize, grasp, go (to work).

grell, harsh, shrill.

greulich, horrid, horrible.

Grimm (-[e]s), *m.*, fury, wrath.

grimmbewehrt, rage-bound.

grob, rude, unmannerly.

Grobian (-s, -e), *m.*, ruffian, clown.

Groll (-[e]s), *m.*, secret anger, pique, grudge.

gross, large, tall, big.

Gruft (-, "e), *f.*, tomb, cavern.

grün, green (*tone*).

Grund (-[e]s, *"*e), *m.*, reason.

grünen, to keep green, flourish.

Grün-Lindenblüt' (*mode*), green linden bloom.

grüssen, to greet, salute, bow.

gucken, to look, peep.

Gunst, *f.*, favor, taste.

Gurt (-[e]s, -e) = **Gürtel,** *m.*, girth, girdle.

Gürtler (-s, -), *m.*, belt-maker.

gut, good, safe, kind, well.

Gut (-[e]s, *"*er), *n.*, good, blessing, estate, treasure.

Güte, *f.*, goodness, kindness, excellence.

gutgefügt, well joined, properly joined.

H

Hab = **Habe,** *f.*, possession.

haben (hatte, gehabt), to have.

Hacke (-, -n), *f.*, heel.

Hader (-s), *m.*, quarrel.

Hag (-[e]s, -e), *m.*, hedgewood, inclosure.

Hageblüh (*mode*), hedge-blossom, hawthorn.

Hageldonnerwetter (-s, -), *n.*, the very deuce, with a vengeance (91, 12).

Hagelwetterschlag (-[e]s, *"*e), *m.*, thunder and lightning; fire and fury.

Hain (-[e]s, -e), *m.*, wood, grove.

Hall (-[e]s, -e), *m.*, echo, resonance.

halt, forsooth, methinks, indeed.

halten (ie, a), to hold, keep, retain ; **doch hält** ... **Haus,** re-

tains enough to pass in a crowd; **gehalten hoch** exalted, nobly holden.

Haltung, *f.*, composure, bearing.

Halunke (-n, -n), *m.*, scoundrel, rogue.

Hammer (-s, *"*), *m.*, hammer.

Hammerstreich (-[e]s, -e), *m.*, hammer's blow.

Hand (-, *"*e), *f.*, hand, handwriting; **zur -,** at hand, ready.

Handlung (-, -en), *f.*, action, deed, act, treatment.

handtieren, to do business, slave.

Handwerker (-s, -), *m.*, artisan, laborer.

Hanf (-[e]s), *m.*, hemp.

hängen, to hang, attach.

Harfe (-, -n), *f.*, harp.

harren, to wait.

hart, hard.

Harte-Tritt (*mode*), hearty kick.

Hase (-n, -n), *m.*, rabbit, hare.

Hass (-es), *m.*, hate, spite.

hastig, quickly, hastily.

hauen (hieb, gehauen), to strike, pound.

Haufe[n] (-ns, -n), *m.*, heap, great numbers; **über'n -n rennen,** to ride rough shod over ... (67, 23); **über'n -n stossen,** to run away with one (100, 22).

Haupt (-es, *"*er), *n.*, head, chief.

Hauptausgang (-[e]s, *"*e), *m.*, main exit.

Hauptschiff (-[e]s, -e), *n.*, nave.

Haus (-es, *"*er), *n.*, house; **zu -,** at home; **nach -,** home, homeward.

heben (o *or* u, o), to raise, lift.

heda! hi! halloo!

Heer (-[e]s, -e), *n.*, host, army.

heftend, fixed, fastened.

heftig, violent.

hegen, to cherish.

hehr, sublime, glorious.

hei! hey! hurrah!

Heil (-[e]s), *n.*, salvation, welfare, good; -! Hail!

Heiland (-[e]s), -e), *m.*, Saviour, Messiah.

heilig, sacred, holy.

heilsaftig, succulent, wholesome.

Heim (-[e]s, -e), *n.*, home.

heimgewandt, turned homeward.

heimisch, native.

heimlich, secretly, mysteriously.

heischen, to desire.

heiser, hoarse, husky, croaking.

heissen (ie, ei), to be named, call, bid.

heiter, genial, bright, merry, pleasure loving, gay.

Held (-en, -en), *m.*, hero, champion.

helfen (a, o), to help, assist; **was hilft's?** what can be done?

hell, light, clear.

her, here.

herab, down.

herab*wenden (wandte, gewandt), to bend down toward, condescend.

heran, this way, come here.

heran*machen, to be up and doing, work toward.

heran*treten (a, e), to advance, approach.

heraus, out, out there.

heraus*kennen (kannte, gekannt), to pick out, know in a crowd.

heraus*kommen (kam, o), to come out, shine out.

heraus*strecken, to stretch (the head) out.

herbei, hither, this way.

herbei*kommen (kam, o), to approach, step up (this way).

Herbst (-[e]s, -e), *m.*, autumn.

Herd (-[e]s, -e), *m.*, hearth, home.

herein, in here, come in!

her*gehen (ging, gegangen), to pass off, take place.

Herold (-[e]s, -e), *m.*, herald.

Herr (-en, -en), *m.*, master, lord.

Herrichtung (-, -en), *f.*, arrangements.

herrje, great heavens! Zounds!

herrlich, lordly, magnificent.

herum*gehen (ging. gegangen), to run about, fancy, have an idea.

hervor*rauschen, to start up.

hervor*rücken, to push before, shove before.

Herz (-ens, -en), *n.*, heart.

Herzbeschwer (-[e]s), *n. and f.*, unhappiness.

Herzensschlag (-[e]s, ˝e), *m.*, beating of the heart, heart-beat.

herzu, hither.

herzu*schaffen, compose so quickly (III, 5-6).

hetzen, to bait, incite.

heut' [heute], to-day.

hie [hier], here.

Hieb (-[e]s, -e), *m.*, blow, stroke.

hienied', here below, forever.

hierher, this way, hither.

hihi! hee hee!

hilf, *see* **helfen.**

Himmel (-s, -), *m.*, heaven, sky.

himmlisch, heavenly.

hin, away, thither.

hinan, up there, up to, 'tis time to go.

hinaus, out, out there; **geht's da –,** that's his scheme?

hinaus*führen, to lead out, to extricate.

hindern, to prevent, restrain, hinder.

Hindernis (-ses, -se), *n.*, obstacle, difficulty.

hinnen, away!

hinter, behind, back of.

hinein*schauen, to look in, investigate, peek in.

hin*geben (a, e), to intrust, confide, calm (jealousy) (108, 35).

hin*gehen (ging, gegangen), to vanish, fly (time).

hineingerannt [rennen], caught, made a mess (of it).

hinken, to limp.

hinweg*sehen (a, e), to look over.

Historie (–, -n), *f.*, history.

hoch, high.

hoch-bedürft'ge, care-ridden.

hochgeehrt, highly honored.

hochgelahrten, most learned.

hochgemut, high-minded.

höchst [hoch], highest.

Hoch-Tannen (*name of a tone*), high-fir-tree.

Hochzeit (–, -en), *f.*, marriage, wedding.

Hochzeitsfest (-[e]s, -e), *n.*, marriage-feast.

Hof (-[e]s, "e), *m.*, court, yard.

hoffen, to hope.

Hoffnung (–, -en), *f.*, hope, expectation, delight.

hoh, *see* **hoch.**

Höhe (–, -n), *f.*, height.

hohl, hollow.

höhnen, to scorn, mock.

höhnisch, scornful, mocking.

hold, kind, sweet, agreeable, heavenly.

holdselig, holdseliglich, graciously, sweetly.

holen, to fetch, bring; **der Teufel ... –,** the devil take.

holla! holla! avast!

Holz (-es, "er), *n.*, wood.

horchen, to listen, hark, hear.

hören, to hear, listen.

hübsch, pretty, good, favorable, stanch (126, 5).

Hügel (-s, –), *m.*, hill.

Huld, *f.*, favor.

huld-geboren, born to favor, destined to grace.

huldigend, in homage.

huldreich, most gracious, most rare.

Hülfe, *f.*, help, assistance.

Hunger (-s), *m.*, hunger.

Hungerleider (-s, –), *m.*, starveling.

hungern, to hunger.

Hungersnot (–, "e), *f.*, famine, starvation.

hüpfen, to hop, flutter.

Hut, *f.*, heed.

I

ich, I.

ihm, (to) him, (to) it.

ihn, him, it.

Ihnen, to you, you.

ihnen, to them, them.

ihr, ye, you; to her, her; to it, it; her, hers, its, their, theirs.

Ihr, you, yours.
im = in dem.
immer, ever, always.
immerdar, always, ever.
immerhin, of course, nevertheless.
in, in, at, into, to.
Inbrunst, *f.*, fervor, vehemence.
Inhalt (-[e]s), *m.*, contents.
innerlich, tenderly, affectionately.
inne, within; – **haben,** to know thoroughly.
inniglich, sincerely.
inwendlich, inside.
ins = in das.
irr, -e, confused, sacred.
irren, to err, be wrong.

J

ja, yes; but, just even, you know.
jagen, to hunt, pursue.
Jahr (-[e]s, -e), *n.*, year.
Jahrhundert (-s, -e), *n.*, century, age.
jährlich, yearly, once a year, anually.
jammern, to trouble, to grieve.
jauchzend, exulting.
je, *adv.*, ever, once, at any time, at all times; – **mehr** – **besser,** the more the better.
je, *contraction of* **jemine,** why! heavens!
jed, -er, each, every.
jemand, (-es) anyone.
jetzt, now.
Johannisfest (-[e]s, -e), *n.*, St. John's festival.
Johannisnacht (–, ˮe), *f.*, midsummer eve.
Jordan (-s), *m.*, Jordan.

Jubel (-s), *m.*, rejoicing, mirth, exultation.
juchhei! hurrah!
jucken, to itch, tingle.
Jugend, *f.*, youth.
jugendheiss, enthusiastic, ardent.
jugendlich, youthful.
Jugendliebe, *f.*, youthful love.
Jugendzeit, *f.*, youth.
jung, young.
Jungfer (–, -n), *f.*, virgin, maid, maiden.
Jungfrau (–, -en), *f.*, maiden, young woman.
Jung-Gesell (-en, -en), *m.*, bachelor.
Junker (-s, –), *m.*, squire, young nobleman; – **Hochmut,** Sir Haughtiness; – **Unkraut,** Sir Good-for-Nothing.

K

Kahn (-[e]s, ˮe), *m.*, boat.
Kälber (*mode*), calf.
kalt, cold; – **machen,** *fig.*, to kill, make shiver, scare.
Kammer (–, -n), *f.*, room, chamber.
Kämmerlein (-s, –), *n.*, chamber, little bedroom.
kathederart, ecclesiastical.
karg, close-fisted, penurious.
kaufen, to buy.
kaum, scarcely.
Kegel (-s, –), *m.*, ninepin.
kehren, to turn.
Keil (-[e]s, -e), *m.*, wedge, club.
Keilerei (–, -en), *f.*, drubbing, row.
kein, none, no one, not one.
Keller (-s, –), *m.*, cellar; drinks.

kennen (kannte, gekannt), to know, be acquainted.

Kenntnis (-, -se), *f.*, knowledge.

Kerl (-[e]s, -e), *m.*, fellow, rogue.

Kies (-es, -e), *m.*, gravel, coarse sand, stone.

Kiesel (-s, -), *m.*, pebbles.

kiesen [küren] (kor, gekoren), to choose, install.

Kind (-[e]s, -er), *n.*, child.

Kind[e]lein (-s, -), *n.*, little child, dear daughter.

kinderlos, childless.

Kindtaufe (-, -n), *f.*, child baptism, family cares.

Kirchenchor (-[e]s, *u*e), *m.*, church choir.

Kirchenraum (-[e]s, *u*e), *m.*, church, altar.

Kirchenstuhlbank (-, *u*e), *f.*, bench, pew.

Klage (-, -n), *f.*, grievance, complaint.

klagen, to complain, lament.

Klageruf (-[e]s, -e), *m.*, complaint.

Klang (-[e]s, *u*e), *m.*, sound, tune; **Kling und Klang,** sound and song.

klappen, to flap, clap.

klar, clear, distinct, clearly.

klärlich, clearly, correctly.

Klausel (-, -n), *f.*, clause, phrase.

kleben, to stick.

Kleb-Silbe (-, -n), *f.*, clipped word, contraction (*see* Introduction).

Kleid (-[e]s, -er), *n.*, clothes, garment.

Kleister (-s), *m.*, paste.

klimpern, to jingle, tinkle, strum.

Kling, *see* **Klang.**

klingen (a, u), to sound, ring.

klingend, *tech.*, dissyllabic (see Introduction).

Klinze [Klinse] (-, -n), chink, hole.

klopfen, to beat, knock.

klug, clever, wise.

Knabe (-n, -n), *m.*, boy, apprentice.

knacken, to crash, break.

knapp, tight.

knappen, to come short.

Knecht (-[e]s, -e), *m.*, servant, porter.

Knieriemen (-s, -), *m.*, knee strap.

Knieriemen-Schlag (*mode*), knee-strap-whack.

knüpfen, to join on, add.

Knüppel (-s, -), *m.*, club, cudgel.

Kobold (-[e]s, -e), *m.*, imp, goblin.

Koloratur (-, -en), *f.*, turns, embellishments, grace notes.

kommen (kam, o), to come.

König (-[e]s, -e), *m.*, king.

können (konnte, gekonnt), to be able, may, can, might.

Konsonanz (-, -en), *f.*, consonance.

Kopf (-[e]s, *u*e), *m.*, head.

Korb (-[e]s, *u*e), *m.*, basket; *coll. expression,* **einem den – geben,** to give the mitten.

Körner, lines rhyming with a line in in the next stanza, (see Introduction).

krächzen, to croak.

Krach (-[e]s, -e), *m.*, crack, crash, crashing.

Kraft (-, *u*e), *f.*, strength, force.

Krähe (-, -n), *f.*, rook, jackdaw.

Krämer [Kramer] (-s, -), *m.*, shopkeeper, grocer.

krank, sick, ill.

Kranz (-es, *u*e), *m.*, wreath, chaplet, prize.

Kränzlein (-s, -), *n.*, wreath, chaplet.

kraus, curly, confused, ruffled.

Kraut (-[e]s, "er), *n.*, weed, cabbage.

Kreide (-, -n), *f.*, chalk.

kreischen, to shriek, squeal, bawl, croak.

Kreis (-es, -e), *m.*, circle.

kriegen, to conquer, get.

Kron[e] (-, -n), *f.*, crown.

krönen, to crown.

Küche (-, -n), *f.*, kitchen, cooking, board, food.

Kuchen (-s, -), *m.*, cakes.

kühl, cool, chilly.

kühn, bold.

kümmern, sich, to concern one's self.

kümmern, to concern, bother, grieve.

kund, known, notorious.

künden, to make known.

Kunst (-, "e), *f.*, art.

Kunstfreund (-[e]s, -e), *m.*, colleague, critic.

Kunstgesang (-[e]s, "e), *m.*, art-song, lyric art.

kunstgewog'ner, art-patron.

Kupferschmied (-[e]s, -e), *m.*, coppersmith.

Kürschner (-s, -), *m.*, furrier.

kurz, short; *also a tone.*

Kurzen-Liebe (*tone*), passing love.

Kuss (-es, "e), *m.*, kiss.

L

labend, refreshing, soothing.

lachen, to laugh.

lachend, laughing, smiling.

lächeln, to smile.

Laden (-s, "), *m.*, store, shop, stall.

laden (u, a), to invite.

lag, *see* **liegen.**

Laie (-n, -n), *m.*, layman, the unlearned; **-n-Ohr,** layman's ear.

Land (-[e]s, "er), *n.*, land, country.

lang, long (*tone*).

Länge (-, -n), *f.*, length; **auf die –,** in the long run.

länger, longer.

längst, long ago, long since.

Lärm (-[e]s), *m.*, noise.

lassen (ie, a), to let, leave, cause; **im Stich –,** leave in the lurch.

Last (-, -en), *f.*, burden, load.

Laster (-s, -), *n.*, vices, crimes (in singing, see Introduction); *tech.,* faulty rhyme.

Laub (-[e]s, "er), *n.*, foliage, leaves.

lauern, to lower, lurk.

Lauf (-[e]s, "e), *m.*, run, course.

laufen (ie, au), to run.

Laune (-, -n), *f.*, mood, humor.

lauschen, to listen; **mir sinnend gab zu –,** have given me to reflect upon.

laut, loud, aloud, loudly.

Laut (-[e]s, -e), *m.*, sound, tone, utterance.

Laute (-, -n), *f.*, lute.

leben, to live.

Leben (-s, -), *n.*, life, existence.

lebend, living.

Lebensbaum (-[e]s, "e), *m.*, tree of life.

Lebensmüh'[e] (-, -n), *f.*, life's troubles.

Leberbaum (-[e]s, "e), *m.*, liver-tree, flesh-tree (Beckmesser's corruption of **Lebensbaum**).

leblos, lifeless, inanimate.

lecken, to lick.

Leder (-s, –), *n.*, leather.

ledig, single, unmarried.

leer, empty; *fig.*, inane.

legen, to lay, put, place.

lehnen, to lean.

Lehnstuhl (-[e]s, ̈e), *m.*, arm chair.

Lehrbube (-n, -n), *m.*, apprentice.

Lehre (–, -n), *f.*, teaching, doctrine, instruction.

lehren, to teach, instruct.

Lehrling (-s, -e), *m.*, pupil, apprentice.

Leib (-[e]s, -er), *m.*, body.

leicht, easy, light.

leichtlich, easily, lightly.

leid, sorrowful; **es ist mir –, es tut mir –,** I am sorry.

Leiden (-s, –), *n.*, affliction, calamity.

leidend, suffering, deplorable, ailing.

leidenschaftlich, passionately, sorrowfully.

leihen (ie, ie), to lend.

Leim (-[e]s, -e), *m.*, glue.

leimen, to glue.

Leimsieder (-s, –), *m.*, glue-boiler.

Leinweber (-s, –), *m.*, linen-weaver.

leise, gently, softly.

Leisten (-s, –), *m.*, last, model.

leisten, to perform, accomplish.

Leiter (–, -n), *f.*, ladder.

lenken, to direct, lead, fashion.

Lenz (-es, -e), *m.*, spring.

Lerchen (*tone*), lark.

lernen, to learn.

lesen (a, e), to read.

letzt, last.

letzt-entbot'ner, last to be called (out of modesty).

leuchten, to gleam, stream.

leuchtend, gleaming, shining.

Leute, *pl.*, people.

Licht (-[e]s, -er), *n.*, light.

licht, clear, luminous, light.

Lichtgiesser (-s, –), *m.*, candlemaker, chandler.

lieb, dear; **einen -haben,** to like; **für etwas – sein,** be favorable to.

Liebe, *f.*, love, affection.

lieben, to love; **geliebt,** beloved.

lieber, rather, sooner.

Liebesfeuer (-s, –), *n.*, passion.

liebesheilig, loved, sacred.

Liebestraum (-[e]s, ̈e), *m.*, love's dream.

lieblich, charming, lovely.

liebselig, blissful.

Lied (-[e]s, -er), *n.*, song.

Liedlein (-s, –), *n.*, little song, ditty.

liegen (a, e), to lie, be situated, be, recline.

lind, calm, soothing, mild.

Linde (–, -n), *f.*, linden tree, lime tree.

Lineal (-[e]s, -e), *n.*, rule, ruler.

Lippe (–, -n), *f.*, lip.

link, left; **-s,** at the left.

Liste (–, -n), *f.*, list.

Lob (-[e]s), *n.*, praise, commendation.

loben, to praise.

Loch (-[e]s, ̈er), *n.*, hole, gap.

Locke (–, -n), *f.*, curl, lock, ringlet.

locken, to allure, entrap.

lockend, alluring.

Lockenhaar (-[e]s, -e), *n.*, curly hair, hair.

Lohn (-[e]s, ˮe), *m.*, reward, payment.

lohnen, to reward, award, pay.

Lorbeerbaum (-[e]s, ˮe), *m.*, laurel tree, tree of victory.

Los (-es, -e), *n.*, lot, lottery, ticket.

los, free, rid.

löschen, *reg.*, to put out, extinguish.

lösen, to relax, loosen.

los*kommen (kam, o), to get rid of.

los*lassen (ie, a), to set free, let alone.

los*sprechen (a, o), to win, release (from apprenticeship), hence to promote.

los*werden (ward *or* wurde, o), to get rid of.

lud, *see* **laden.**

lud ein, *see* **einladen.**

Luft (-, ˮe), *f.*, air.

luftig, airy, dizzy.

Lug und Trug, lies and fraud.

lugend, watching, spying.

Lümmel (-s, -), *m.*, lubber, clown.

Lungerer (-s, -), *m.*, lounger.

Lust (-, ˮe), *f.*, delight, desire, laughter, happiness, fun (129, 12).

Lustgelag (-[e]s, -e), *n.*, merrybout, convivial amusement.

lustig, merry, gay.

Lustverlangen (-s), *n.*, love's desire.

M

machen, to make, do.

mächtig, powerful, intensely.

Mädchen (-s, -), *n.*, girl, maid.

Mädchenherz (-ens, -en), *n.*, maiden's heart.

Mädel = **Mädchen.**

mag, *see* **mögen.**

Mägd[e]lein (-s, -), *n.*, maid, maiden.

mahnen, to remind, warn.

Mai (-[e]s, -en), *m.*, (month of) May.

Maid, *f.*, maid.

Majestät (-, -en), *f.*, pomp, majesty.

Mal (-[e]s, -e), *n.*, time, occasion.

malen, to paint.

man, one, they, *indef.*

manch, many, many a.

mangelhaft, faulty.

Mann (-[e]s, ˮer), *m.*, man, husband.

Mannsen, *pl.*, *vulg.*, men, males.

Mauer (-, -n), *f.*, wall, masonry.

Markt (-[e]s, ˮe), *m.*, market-place.

Marschall (-[e]s, ˮe), *m.*, marshal.

Mass (-es, -e), *n.*, time, measure.

Massabzwacker (-s, -), *m.*, false measurer.

Maul (-[e]s, ˮer), *n.*, *vulg.*, tongue, mouth, noise.

meckern, to bleat.

Meer (-[e]s, -e), *n.*, sea, ocean.

mehr, more.

mein, mine ; *exclamation*, pray ! gracious ! (*cf.* oh my !)

meinen, to think, mean, have the opinion, feel.

meinethalb[en], on my account, as far as I am concerned.

Meiran, *mode*, marjoram.

Meise (-, -n), *f.*, titmouse, chickadee.

meist, most.

Meister (-s, -), *m.*, master.

Meisterbuhle (-n, -n), *m.*, master-lover.

Meistergericht (-[e]s, -e), *n.*, tribunal.

Meisterin (-, -nen), *f.*, mistress, madam.

Meisterkunst (-, "e), *f.*, master's art.

Meisterlied (-[e]s, -er), *n.*, master-song.

Meisterlohn (-[e]s, "e), *m.*, title of master.

Meister-Pracht, *f.*, master's ability.

Meisterregeln, *f.*, master rules.

Meistersang (-[e]s), *m.*, master-song.

Meister-Schlag (-[e]s, "e), *m.*, (the stroke by which one is awarded the) master's title.

Meistersinger (-s, -), *m.*, master-singer.

Meister-Ton (-[e]s, "e), *m.*, master-mode.

Meistertum (-[e]s, "er), *n.*, master-hood, mastership.

Meister-Wahn (-[e]s), *m.*, master fancy, delusion.

Meisterweise (-, -n), *f.*, master-mode, master-song.

Meister-Zunft (-, "e), *f.*, master's guild.

melden, to announce.

Melissenblümlein, *mode*, sugar-loaf-flower.

Melodei (-, -en), *f.*, melody.

memorieren, to memorize, learn by heart.

Mensch (-en, -en), *m.*, mortal, human being, man.

Menschenleib (-[e]s, -er), *m.*, human body; **dass ob den Fuss**

am —, on account of people's feet.

Merk (-[e]s, -e), *n.*, sign, criterion, thought, attention.

merken, to note, mark, notice.

Merker (-s, -), *m.*, judge, marker.

Merkerschuh (-[e]s, -e), *m.*, marker's shoe.

Merkersprüchlein (-s, -), *n.*, marker's verse.

Merkerwahl (-, -en), *f.*, choice of marker.

Merkerzeichen (s, -), *n.*, marker's insignia, hammer.

merkwürdig, remarkable.

messen (a, e), to measure.

Metzger (-s, -), *m.*, butcher.

Meuterei (-, -en), *f.*, mutiny.

mich, me.

Miene (-, -n), *f.*, mien, bearing.

mild, mild, gentle.

mindern, to diminish, grow less.

minnig, loving, affectionate.

minniglich, kind, loving.

mir, to me, me; **es ist** —, it seems, **es war** —, I thought.

Mischgebräu (-[e]s, -e), *n.*, hodge-podge.

Missbehagen (-s), *n.*, dissatisfaction, displeasure.

Missetat (-, -en), *f.*, misdeed, offense.

mit, with, in, along with, in company with.

Mitte, *f.*, middle, midst; *fig.*, means.

mocht, *see* **mögen.**

möchte [mögen], **ich** —, I would like.

mögen (mochte, gemocht *or* mögen), may, might; to like, care.

möglich, possible.

Morgen (-s, -), *m.*, morning.

morgen, to-morrow.

Morgenglüh'n (-s), *n.*, morning glow.

morgen[d]lich, morning-like, matutinal.

Morgenröt', *f.*, morning red, flush of morning.

morgens, in the morning, of the morning.

Morgentraum (-[e]s, ⁎e), *m.*, morning dream.

Mühe (-, -n), *f.*, trouble, pains, labor.

Mund (-[e]s, -e *or* ⁎er), *m.*, mouth.

munter, cheerful, brisk, lively, gay.

Muskatennuss (-, ⁎e), *f.*, nutmeg, spice.

Muse (-, -n), *f.*, muse.

Musikant (-en, -en), *m.*, strolling player.

müssen (musste, gemusst), to be compelled, be obliged.

Müssen, *n.*, *verbal noun,* compulsion.

Muster (-s, -), *n.*, type, sample, model.

Mut (-es), *m.*, courage, mettle, mood, spirit.

Milbe (-, -n), *f.*, abbreviation, the omission of the last syllable of a word (see Introduction).

Myrte (-, -n), *f.*, myrtle.

N

nach, toward, after, according to, to, into, for; -- **Pech riechen,** to smell of pitch (117, 8).

Nachbar (-s, -n), *m.*, neighbor.

nach*lassen (ie, a), to yield, give in.

nach*laufen (ie, au) to run after, follow.

nach*singen (a, u), to imitate in singing, repeat.

nach*stellen, to have designs on.

Nacht (-, ⁎e), *f.*, night; -s, *adv. noun,* at night.

Nachtgewand (-[e]s, -e *or* ⁎er), *n.*, night garment.

nächtig, gloomy, sombre.

Nachtigall (-, -en), *f.*, nightingale; *also a mode.*

nächtlich, night, nightlike, by night.

Nachtwächterhorn (-[e]s, ⁎er), *n.*, night-watchman's horn.

nach*zählen, to count after *or* over.

nah, near.

Nähe, *f.*, neighborhood, proximity.

nahe*liegen (a, e), to lie near by, be fitting.

nahen, to approach, draw near.

nähern, sich, to draw nearer.

Naht (-, ⁎e), *f.*, seam, sewing, sole (115, 2).

nah*treten (a, e), to draw near, approach, resemble.

Name[n] (ns, -n), *m.*, name.

Namenstag (-[e]s, -e), *m.*, christening day.

namentlich, especially, by name.

Narr (-en, -en), *m.*, fool, booby.

naschen, to munch, eat daintily, eat illicitly.

Nase (-, -n), *f.*, nose.

näselnd, snuffling.

Nass (-es), *n.*, dew (of a fountain).

nass, wet, moist.

Natur, *f.*, nature.

Nebenbuhler (-s, -), *m.*, rival.

nehmen (a, genommen), to take.

Neid (-[e]s), *m.*, envy, jealousy.

neidisch, envious.

neigen, to incline, bow, stay, descend; **geneigt,** well disposed.

nein, no.

Nenn' = **Nennung,** *f.*, calling.

nennen (nannte, genannt), to call.

Nest (-[e]s, -er), *n.*, nest.

netzend, moistening, anointing.

neu, fresh, new; **neuen,** recent times (125, 23).

neugierig, curious.

neulich, recently, lately.

neun, nine.

nicht, not; **-s,** nothing.

nicken, to nod.

nie, niemals, never.

nieder, low, lowly down.

nieder*knieen, to kneel down.

nieder*lassen (ie, a), **sich,** to be seated, let down.

nieder*schlagen (u, a), to knock down, whip (in a fight).

nieder*singen (a, u), to outsing, defeat.

niemand, none, no one.

nimm, *see* **nehmen.**

nimm . . . an, *see* **annehmen.**

Nische (-, -n), *f.*, niche, recess.

noch, yet, until, now, still, further, nor; **ja dahin hat's - lange Ruh'!** thus far I have already progressed.

Not (-, "e), *f.*, need, necessity, trouble.

nötig, necessary.

Nottaufe (-, -n), *f.*, emergency baptism.

Null (-, -en), *f.*, zero, nothing.

nun, now, well.

nur, only, solely, but just.

Nür[e]nberg, Nuremburg.

Nutz (-es), *m.*, use, good.

nützen, to make use of, avail.

O

ob, whether, on account of, if, concerning, although, on.

oben, above.

Occident (-[e]s), *m.*, west, occident.

oder, or.

offen, open.

öffnen, to open.

oft, often, frequently.

ohne, without.

ohnmächtig, weak, fainting.

Opfer (-s, -), *n.*, offering, sacrifice.

Opfertod (-[e]s), *m.*, sacrifice.

ordentlich, regularly.

Ort (-[e]s, -e *or* "er), *m.*, place, seat.

P

Paar (-[e]s, -e), *n.*, pair, couple, brace; **ein paar,** *vulg.*, some, few.

packen, to grasp.

Panier (-[e]s, -e), *n.*, banner, standard.

Papier (-[e]s, -e), *n.*, paper.

Paradies (-es, -e), *n.*, paradise.

paradiesisch, paradisal, celestial.

Parnass (-es), *m.*, Parnassus.

passen, to fit, suit, be appropriate.

passieren, to happen, occur.

Pause (-, -n), *f.*, pause, intermission; (for special meaning consult Introduction, p. 11).

pausieren, to pause, rest.

Pech (-[e]s), *n.*, pitch; *fig.*, misfortune.

Pein, *f.*, pain, alas!

Person (-, -en), *f.*, person, character.

Persönlichkeit (-, -en), *f.*, personality.

Pfad (-[e]s, -e), *m.*, path, way.

Pfeffer (-s), *m.*, pepper.

Pferd (-[e]s. -e), *n.*, horse.

Popularität, *f.*, popularity.

Posse (-, -n), *f.*, drollery, jest, buffoonery.

Pracht, *f.*, magnificence, pomp, talent, splendor.

prangen, to shine in splendor, make a show.

Prangen (-s), *n.*, splendor.

Pranger (-s, -), *m.*, pillory, whipping-post.

Preis (-es, -e), *m.*, prize, glory.

preisen (ie, ie), to praise, commend.

Preisverderber (-s, -), *m.*, price-cutter, scab.

pressieren, to be urgent; **pressiert's den Herrn?** is the gentleman pressed (for time)?

Probe (-, -n), *f.*, test, rehearsal.

probieren, to try, attempt, try on (a shoe).

Prosodie, *f.*, prosody, poetry.

Prügel (-s, -), *m.*, club, cudgel.

Prügel-Färbeblau, bruises, black and blue.

Prügelei (-, -en), *f.*, fight, rumpus.

prügeln, to whip, fight.

Pult (-[e]s, -e), *n.*, desk.

Punkt (-[e]s, -e), *m.*, point, matter.

pure, pure, simple.

putzen, to dress up, ad

Q

Qual (-, -en), *f.*, pain, love, grief.

quälen, sich, to torment, enrage, roil.

Quartier (-s, -e), *n.*, lodgings, quarter.

Quell (-[e]s, -e), *m.*, source, well, fountain.

Quelle (-, -n), *f.*, source, well, fountain.

quer, across.

R

Rabe (-n, -n), *m.*, raven.

Racker (-s, -), *m.*, villain, cur.

Rahmen (-s, -), *m.*, sole leather, welts, welted sole.

rammeln, to tramp down, ram.

Rand (-[e]s, *"*er) *m.*, edge.

Rank (-[e]s, *"*e), *m.*, trick, wile.

rasch, quickly, sudden, swift.

rasend, raving, frantic.

Rasenstück (-[e]s, -e), *n.*, sod, turf.

Rat (-[e]s, *"*e), *m.*, council, councilors; cure *or* help (115, 3).

raten (ie, a), to advise, counsel, guess, hit upon.

raufen, to fight, scuffle.

Raum (-[e]s, *"*e), *m.*, space, room, restraint.

rauschen, to bustle, war, glitter, swoop, murmur.

räuspern, sich, to clear the throat.

recht, right, good; **was -s,** worth hearing (61, 12).

rechts, at the right.

Recke (-n, -n), *m.*, giant, hero; **Dichter-,** hero-poet.

recken, sich, to rack, torment.

reden, to talk, speak; **sich – lassen,** to lay one's self open.

Regel (–, -n), *f.*, rule, principle.

regen, sich, to be stirring.

Regenbogen (-s, –), *m.*, (*mode*), rainbow.

regnen, to rain.

reiben (ie, ie), to rub.

reich, rich, handsome.

Reich (-[e]s, -e), *n.*, empire, realm, kingdom.

reichen, to give, bestow, reach.

reichlich, richly, in great measure.

reif, ripe.

Reihe [Reigen] (–, -n), *f.*, rows, series, figure.

Reihentanz (-es, *ǔ*e), *m.*, circular-dance.

Reim (-[e]s, -e), *m.*, rhyme.

reimen, sich, to rhyme, fit, agree.

rein, pure, clean; **ein Engel –,** a regular angel.

Reis (-es, -er), *n.*, prize, sprig.

reisen, to travel, rove.

reissen (i, i), to tear.

reizen, to irritate, provoke.

rennen (rannte, gerannt), to run.

Respekt (-[e]s), *m.*, respect, regard.

respektabel, honorable.

Reue, *f.*, repentance, regret.

reuen, sich, to repent; **die Probe nicht –,** to stand the test.

Richt', *f.*, row, range, line (of); **was euch zum Liede – und Schnur,** all that belongs to a properly constructed song.

richten, to direct, turn, guide; *cf. military term*, **richtet euch,** right dress; **wenn du schön gericht',** when you are finely dressed.

Richter (-s, –), *m.*, judge.

richtig, correct, right, proper.

riechen (o, o), to smell.

Ring (-[e]s, -e), *m.*, ring, circle.

Ringel (-s, –), *m.*, ring, circle.

rings, in circles, around.

Ritter (-s, –), *m.*, knight.

Rittersporn (-[e]s, -e), *m.*, (...**sporen** (-s, –), *m.*, (*mode*), knight-spur.

römisch, Roman.

Rosen (*tone*), rose.

rosig, roseate, rosy.

Rosmarin (*mode*), rosmary.

Ross (-es, -e), *n.*, horse, steed.

rot, red, reddish.

rotbrünstig, burning red.

rotten, sich, to collect, conspire.

Rücken (-s, –), *m.*, back.

rücken, to move, hitch along; **Ort und Zeit nah –,** to be opportune.

Ruf (-[e]s, -e), *m.*, cry, call, summons.

rufen (ie, u), to call, summon.

Ruhe, *f.*, composure, rest, repose.

ruhen, to rest, sleep.

Ruhm (-[e]s), *m.*, glory, fame.

rühmen, to boast, celebrate, hail, claim.

ruhmerkoren, elected to fame (116, 8).

rühren, to move, touch; **gerührt,** with emotion.

runzeln, to wrinkle.

S

sacht, slowly.

Sack (-[e]s, *ǔ*e), *m.*, bag, sack, baggage.

Sakristei (–, -en), *f.*, sacristy.

sagen, to say, tell, relate.

sammeln, sich, to gather (itself).

Sammlung (-, -en), *f.*, consideration, time to collect one's self.

sanft, gentle, tenderly.

Sang (-[e]s, *"*e), *m.*, song.

Sänger (-s, -), *m.*, singer (by profession).

Sankt, *Lat.*, saint.

satt, satisfied, full, tired of.

Satz (-es, *"*e), *m.*, movement, sentence.

sauer, sour, unpleasant, disagreeable.

saugen (o,o), to suck, drink (105, 14).

Säule (-, -n), *f.*, pillar, column.

Saum (-[e]s, *"*e), *m.*, seam, hedge, crown (of foliage).

Schacher (-s), *m.*, bartering, dicker.

Schade[n] (-ns, *"*n), *m.*, sorrow, harm, disgrace.

schädlich, harmful, pernicious.

schaffen (schuf, a) *and reg.*, procure, create, kindle; compose; find *or* manage (115, 3), bring (118, 21).

Schäffler (-s, -), *m.*, cooper, tub-maker.

schallen, peal, resound.

schämen, to shame; **sich -,** to be embarrassed.

Schande, *f.*, shame, disgrace.

schändlich, shameful, disgraceful.

Schandlied (-[e]s, -er), *n.*, insulting song.

Schanze (-, -n), *f.*, redoubt, court.

scharf, sharp.

Schätzel = Schatz (-es, *"*e), *m.*, beau, sweetheart, treasure.

schätzen, to prize, treasure.

schauen, to look, behold.

Schein (-[e]s, -e), *m.*, light, shine.

scheinbar, seemingly, apparently.

scheinen (ie, ie), to shine, appear, seem.

Schelle (-, -n), *f.*, bell; *vulg.*, box on the ear.

Schelm (-[e]s, -e), *m.*, rogue, rascal.

schelten (a, o), to scold.

Schemel (-s, -), *m.*, stool, footstool.

schenken, to present, give as a present.

scheren (o, o), to shave, shear, cut; **sich -,** depart, withdraw.

Scherz (-es, -e), *m.*, joke.

scheuen, to avoid, shun.

schicken, to send; **sich -,** be appropriate.

schier, clear, neat, completely.

Schild (-[e]s, -e), *m.*, shield.

schinden (u, u), **sich,** to drudge, to slave.

Schläfe (-, -n), *f.*, temple, forehead.

schlafen (ie, a), to sleep.

Schlafenzeit, *f.*, time to sleep.

Schlag (-[e]s, *"*e), *m.*, stroke, blow; *fig.*, word, song.

schlagen (u, a), to strike, pound, hit.

Schlägerei (-, -en), *f.*, blows, scuffle.

Schlagreim (-[e]s, -e), *m.*, whack-rhyme (31, 19).

schlängeln, to wind.

schlank, slender, shapely.

schlappen, to flap, flare, open.

schlecht, bad, poor (taste), tawdry (33, 17).

schleichen (i, i), to creep, steal upon.

Schleuder (–, n), *f.*, sling.

schliessen (o, o), to close, shut.

schliesslich, finally, eventually.

schlimm, bad, troublesome.

Schloss (-es, "er), *n.*, castle, palace.

Schlosser (-s, –), *m.*, locksmith.

schluchzend, sobbing.

Schluss (-es, "e), *m.*, conclusion, end.

Schmach, *f.*, ignominy, disgrace.

schmähen, to abuse, bring to shame.

schmal, narrow.

schmecken, to taste.

Schmerz (-ens *or* es, -en), *m.*, pain, smart.

schmerzen, to pain, give pain.

Schmied (-[e]s, -e), *m.*, blacksmith.

Schmiere [Schmierich] (–, -en), *f.*, grease, salve.

schmücken, to adorn, dress up.

Schnabel (-s, "), *m.*, bill, beak; *vulg.*, mouth, throat.

Schnauze (–, -n), *f.*, snout, muzzle.

Schnecken (*tone*), snail.

Schneider (-s, –), *m.*, tailor.

schnell, quickly, sudden.

Schnur (–, -en *or* "e), *f.*, lacing, cord, string (*see* **Richt'**).

schon, already, doubtless, even; – **gut,** all right.

schön, lovely, beautiful, good; *vulg.*, all right.

Schoss (-es, "e), *m.*, lap.

schräg, oblique.

Schrank (-[e]s, "e), *m.*, sideboard, pantry, cupboard.

schreiben (ie, ie), to write, compose.

Schreiber (-s, –), *m.*, clerk, scribe.

Schreib-Papier (*mode*), writing paper.

schreien (ie, ie), to shriek, howl.

Schreien (-s), *n.*, howling, shrieking.

Schrein (-[e]s, -e), *m.*, box, chest, cupboard.

Schreiner (-s, –), *m.*, joiner.

schreiten (schritt, geschritten), to step, proceed.

Schrift (–, -en), *f.*, writing.

Schritt (-[e]s, -e), *m.*, step, tramp, stride.

Schrollen, *tech.*, faulty rhyme.

schüchtern, shy, timidly.

Schuh (-[e]s, -e), *m.*, shoe.

Schuhwerk (-[e]s, -e), *n.*, supply of shoes; shoe business.

Schuld (–, -en), *f.*, crime, fault, guilt.

schulden, to owe.

Schüler (-s, –), *m.*, scholar.

Schulfreund (-[e]s, -e), *m.*, schoolman.

Schuhmacherei (–, -en), *f.*, shoe-making.

Schurz (-es, -e), *m.*, lap, apron.

Schuss (-es, "e), *m.*, shot, shooting.

Schuster (-s, –), *m.*, cobbler.

schusterlich, cobbler-fashion.

schustern, to cobble.

Schuster-Stuben, *pl.*, *f.*, cobbler's shop.

Schutz (-es), *m.*, defense, protection.

schwach, weak.

Schwäche (–, -n), *f.*, weakness, failing, fault.

Schwall (-[e]s), *m.*, great quantity, rush, roar; **entnahmt ihr**

'was der Worte -? did you get the meaning of the words?

Schwank (-[e]s, ˝e), *m.*, merry tale, comedy, farce, jest, cunning tricks.

schwanken, to totter.

Schwänken, *see* **Schwank** *above, last meaning.*

Schwarz-Dinten (*mode*), black ink.

schwatzen, to chatter, babble.

schweben, to hover, soar.

schweigen (ie, ie), to be silent.

Schweiss (-es), *m.*, perspiration.

schwellen (o, o), to swell, expand, fill.

schwenken, to wave, swing.

schwer, severe, hard, heavy, sore.

Schwert (-[e]s, -er), *n.*, sword.

schwingen (a, u), to flourish, brandish, swing.

schwören (o, o), to swear, take oath; like (34, 8).

schwül, close, oppressive.

seelenvoll, tenderly, soulful.

Segen (-s, -), *m.*, blessing, bliss.

segnend, in blessing.

sehen (a, e), to see.

sei, *see* **sein.**

Seide (-, -n), *f.*, silk.

Seidenfäden, *pl.*, *m.*, silken thread.

sein, his, its.

sein (war, gewesen), to be, exist.

seit, since, for, for the last, for a number of.

Seite (-, -n), *f.*, side.

selbig, the same.

selbst, even, self, himself.

selbstig, characteristic, own, distinguished.

selig, blessed, glorious.

Selige · Morgentraumdeut -Weise (*mode*), glorious-morning-dreams-true-story.

selten, strange, unusual.

seltsam, rare, strange.

setzen, to put, place, set; **sich -,** take a seat, be seated; **es setzt,** *vulg.*, there is, there are.

seufzen, to sigh.

Seufzer (-s, -), *m.*, sigh.

sich, (to) himself, (to) herself, (to) themselves, (to) itself.

sicher, sure, safe, for certain.

sicherlich, surely.

sichtbar, visible.

sie, it, she, they, them, her.

Sie, you.

sieben, seven.

Sieg (-[e]s, -e), *m.*, victory, triumph.

siegen, to conquer, overcome.

Sieger (-s, -), *m.*, victor, winner.

Siegespreis (-es, -e), *m.*, victor's prize.

Silbe (-, -n), *f.*, syllable, sound, word.

Silentium (-s), *n.*, silence.

sing[e]bar, singable, adapted to the voice.

singen (a, u), to sing; **zu paaren -,** defeat (in singing).

Singer (-s, -), *m.*, singer.

Sing-Gericht (-[e]s, -e), *n.*, song tribunal, song trial.

Singkunst (-, ˝e), *f.*, art of singing.

Singschule (-, -n), *f.*, song class.

Singstunde (-, -n), *f.*, singing lesson.

Sinn (-[e]s, -e), *m.*, sense, mind; **von -en,** out of his senses.

sinnen (a, o), to think, reflect.

Sitte (-, -n), *f.*, custom, manner.

sittig, well-bred, modest.

Sitz (-es, -e), *m.*, seat, chair, pew.

sitzen (sass, gesessen), to sit, fit; **hier sitzt's,** here it is.

Sitzung (–, -en), *f.*, sitting, session, meeting.

Skandal (-[e]s, -e), *m.*, scandal, disgrace.

so, so, there, indeed.

sobald, when, as soon as.

sogleich, immediately.

Sohle (–, -n), *f.*, sole.

Söhnlein (-s, –), *n.*, little son.

solch, such, such a.

sollen, to be obliged (shall, ought); **was soll's?** well? what is it? what do you mean?

Sommer (-s, –), *m.*, summer.

sonderbar, strange, singular.

Sonne (–, -n), *f.*, sun.

sonst, otherwise, else.

Sorge (–, -n), *f.*, care, pains, anxiety.

soviel, so much, as much, to such an extent.

spähen, to peek, to spy.

Spange (–, -n), *f.*, brooch, scarf-pin.

Spann (-[e]s, -e), *m.*, sole, instep.

sparen, to save, spare.

Spass (-es, "e), *m.*, fun, sport, joke.

spät, late.

Spengler (-s, –), *m.*, buckle-maker.

Speer (-[e]s, -e), *m.*, spear.

Spiel (-[e]s, -e), *n.*, play, game.

spielen, to play.

Spitzbube (-n, -n), *m.*, rogue, rascal.

spitzen, to point, open wide.

Spott (-[e]s), *m.*, derision, mocking.

sprechen (a, o), to talk, speak.

spreizen, to spread open; *fig.*, **sich –,** boast.

springen (a, u), to spring, jump.

Spross (-es, -e), *m.*, **Sprosse** (–, -n), *f.*, shoot, sprout; *fig.*, offspring, descendant.

Spruch (-[e]s, "e), *m.*, speech, song, verse, decree, award.

Sprüchlein (-s, –), *n.*, verse, proverb, toast.

Spruchsprecher (-s, –), *m.*, spokesman, speaker.

Sprung (-[e]s, "e), *m.*, bound, leap, jump.

Spucke (–, -n), *f.*, spittle.

Spuk (-[e]s, -e), *m.*, spook, ghost, noise.

spuken, to create a disturbance, haunt.

Spur (–, -en), *f.*, trace, sign, tendency.

stack = stak, *see* **stecken.**

Stadt (–, "e), *f.*, city.

Stadtpfeifer (-s, –), *m.*, town piper.

Stadtschreiber (-s, –), *m.*, town clerk.

Stadtwall (-[e]s, "e), *m.*, city wall, ramparts.

Stamm (-[e]s, "e), *m.*, stock, stem, race.

Stand (-[e]s, "e), *m.*, position, standing, rank.

stark, strong.

Stärke, *f.*, strength, power.

starren, to stare.

Statt, *f.*, place, rank.

statt, instead (of).

stattlich, stately, magnificent.

stecken, *also* **stecken** (stak *or* steckte, gesteckt), *rarely strong*, to put into, stick, be, be concealed.

stehen (stand, gestanden), to stand, be, stop; **da steht's bitter,** it is not well with him; – **bleiben,** to stand still.

stehlen (a, o), to steal.

steif, stiff, hard.

Steige (–, -n), *f.*, stile, elevation.

steigen (ie, ie), to mount, climb, rise.

steil, steep.

Stein (-[e]s, -e), *m.*, stone.

Stelle (–, -n), *f.*, place, spot.

stellen, to place, appoint, decree.

stemmen, to prop; **zu Hauf –,** collect in crowds.

sterben (a, o), to die.

Stern (-[e]s, -e), *m.*, star.

Sternenheer (-[e]s, -e), *n.*, starry host.

Sternenkranz (-es, "e), *m.*, wreath of stars.

stets, always.

Stich (-[e]s, -e), *m.*, puncture, hole; **einen im – lassen,** to leave in the lurch.

Stiefel (-s, – [-n]), *m.*, boot.

Stieglitz (-es, -e), (*mode*), goldfinch.

still, quiet, still, secretly, in secret.

Stimme (–, -n), *f.*, voice.

stimmen, to vote.

stocken, to choke.

Stoff (-[e]s, -e), *m.*, material, stuff, theme. [strophe.

Stolle (-n, -n), *m. and f.*, stanza,

stolz, proud, haughty, exalted.

Stolz-Jüngling (-[e]s -e), *m.*, proud youth; *also a tone.*

stopfen, to stamp, stop.

stören, to disturb.

Stoss (-es, "e), *m.*, thrust, push.

stossen (ie, o), to stub, push; – **auf,** come upon, strike at.

Strafe (–, -n), *f.*, punishment.

Strahl (-[e]s, -en), *m.*, beam, ray.

strahlen, to gleam, glitter.

Strasse (–, -n), *f.*, street.

straucheln, to stumble, make a false step.

strecken, to stretch, work at.

Streich (-[e]s, -e), *m.*, stroke, blow; *fig.*, trick, joke, event; times (133, 31).

streicheln, to sooth, stroke.

streichen (i, i), to stroke, alter, nullify.

Streit (-[e]s), *m.*, strife, contention.

streiten (stritt, gestritten), to dispute, contend.

streng, severe, critical.

Strich (-[e]s, -e), *m.*, stroke, mark, mistake.

Strohhalm (-[e]s, -e), (*mode*), strawblade.

Strumpfwirker (-s, –), *m.*, stockingmaker.

studieren, to study.

Stück (-[e]s, -e), *n.*, piece, story.

Stufe (–, -n), *f.*, step.

Stuhl (-[e]s, "e), *m.*, chair.

Stümper (-s, –), *m.*, fool, bungler.

stumm, dumb, silent.

stumpf, dull, obscure, monosyllabic.

Stunde (–, -n), *f.*, hour; **zur –,** directly.

stürzen, to rush.

suchen, to seek, look for.

summen, to hum, buzz.

Sünderin (–, -nen), *f.*, sinner.

Süss[e], (*tone*), sweet.

T

Tabulatur (-, -en), *f.*, master-singer's code.

Tadel (-s, -), *n.*, blame, fault, blemish.

Tafel (-, -n), *f.*, table, blackboard, slab.

Tag (-[e]s, -e), *m.*, day.

Tagesordnung (-, -en), *f.*, day's program, order of the day.

täglich, daily.

Takt (-[e]s, -e), *m.*, rhythm, beat; **euch bring' ich doch sicher aus dem** –, I'll surely get even with you.

Tal (-[e]s, "er), *n.*, valley.

Tand (-[e]s), *m.*, prattle, nonsense.

Tanz (-[e]s, "e), *m.*, dance.

tanzen, to dance.

Tasche (-, -n), *f.*, basket, handbag, pocket, receptacle.

Tat (-, -en), *f.*, deed.

tät, *from* **tun; tät ... wecken = weckte; tät ... gelingen = gelänge.**

Täubchen (-s, -), *n.*, little bird, little dove.

Täublein (-s, -), *n.*, dove, little bird.

Taufe (-, -n), *f.*, baptism.

taufen, to baptize.

Täufer (-s, -), *m.*, baptizer, interceder.

taugen, to amount to something.

taumeln, to stagger.

täuschen, to deceive, disappoint.

teilen, to share, divide.

Teilnahme, *f.*, sympathy, interest.

Teller (-s, -), *m.*, plate.

teuer, dear.

Teufel (-s, -), *m.*, devil.

tief, deep, low.

Tisch (-[e]s, -e), *m.*, table.

toben, to storm, bluster.

Tochter (-, "), *f.*, daughter.

Tod (-[e]s), *m.*, death.

toll, mad.

Ton (-[e]s, "e), *m.*, tone, scheme of versification.

Töne-Geleis, *n.*, series of tones.

tönen, to utter tone, ring.

Topf (-[e]s, "e), *m.*, pot.

Tor (-[e]s, -e), *n.*, gate.

Tor (-en, -en), *m.*, fool.

töricht [**törig**], foolish, silly.

tosen, to war, rage.

tot, dead.

trachten, to endeavor, strive.

träge, lazy, sluggish.

tragen (u, a), to carry, bear.

Traum (-[e]s, "e), *m.*, dream, vision.

Traumbild (-[e]s, -er), *n.*, dream-picture, vision.

träumen, to dream, sleep.

traurig, sad.

traut, dear.

treffen (traf, o), to hit, correspond, meet, compose.

treiben (ie, ie), to do, drive, perpetrate (a joke), indulge, pound, beat.

trennen, to separate.

Treppe (-, -n), *f.*, flight of stairs, stairs.

treten (a, e), to step, tread.

treu, true, honest, loyal.

Treu[e], *f.*, faithfulness, honesty, loyalty.

Treu-Pelikan (*mode*), true pelican.

Trieb (-[e]s, -e), *m.*, impulse, driving.

Trost (-[e]s, *m.*, consolation, comfort.

Trostlosigkeit, *f.*, despair, comfortlessness.

trotz, in spite of, notwithstanding.

trübe, gloomy, sad.

trüben, to trouble, bias, becloud.

Trunkenbold (-[e]s, -e), *m.*, drunkard.

Tuch (-[e]s, "er), *n.*, cloth, handkerchief.

Trutz [Trotz] (-es), *m.*, defiance, spite.

Tuchscherer (-s, -), *m.*, cloth cutter.

tüchtig, capable, plenty.

tückisch, malicious, deceitful.

tun (tat, a), to do.

U

übel, bad, evil.

üben, to exercise, fulfill (an office).

über, over, concerning, across.

überall, everywhere.

überdenken (überdachte, überdacht), to think over, consider.

überein*stimmen, to agree, coincide, consent.

Überfall (-s, "e), *m.*, sudden start.

über*kegeln, to topple over.

überlang (*tone*), extra long.

Übermacht (-, "e), *f.*, superiority, boundless might.

übermütig, wild, haughty, supercilious.

überragend, towering above.

überrasch[e]t, surprised.

über*schnappen, gasp, crack.

überspringen (a, u), overlap, skip.

übertäuben, to overpower, drown out.

übertrieben, exaggerated.

übrig, remaining, left.

Ufer (-s, -), *n.*, bank, riverside.

Uferrand (-[e]s, "er), *m.*, shore, bank.

um, about, near, around, for; – **zu,** in order to.

um*bringen (brachte, gebracht), to kill, deprive of life.

umdämmern, to surround by darkness.

um*fallen (fiel, a), to tumble over, fall down.

umfassen, to embrace.

umgeben (a, e), to surround.

um*kehren, to turn around.

um*kleiden, sich, to change the clothes.

umrauschen, concealed, arrayed in.

um*schauen, to look around, look sharper (*with* **besser**).

umschliessen (o, o), to inclose, close around.

umsonst, in vain, for nothing.

umstrahlen, to surround with light, shine around; **umstrahlt,** *adj.*, radiant.

um*weben (o, o), to weave about, steal upon.

um*wenden (wandte, gewandt), to turn round, reverse, invert.

umzingeln, to surround, encircle.

unbeirrt, without worry, unworried, with assurance, without wandering.

unermesslich, unmeasurable, measureless.

unablässig, continually.

unbelehrt, not learned, untaught, undisciplined.

unbemerkt, unnoticed, unperceived.

unbenommen, black-balled, refused.

unbeweglich, motionless.

unbewusst, unconsciously.

und, and.

unfasern, to fuzz up, unravel.

Ungeduld, *f.,* impatience.

ungehört, unheard, not listened to.

Ungemach (-[e]s, *"*er), *n.,* vexation, affliction, trouble.

ungestört, undisturbed.

ungewohnt, unaccustomed.

Unglück (-[e]s, -e), *n.,* ill fortune, misfortune, unhappiness, ill.

Unheil (-[e]s, -e), *n.,* evil.

unklar, obscure, not clear; **-e Wort',** obscure words.

Unkraut (-[e]s, *"*er), *n.,* weed.

unmutig, discouraging, displeased.

unnütze[n], useless.

unredbar, unsingable; **-e Worte,** unvocal phrases.

unruhig, uneasy, restless.

unsinnig, senseless, nonsensical.

uns, us, to us, ourselves.

unser, of us, our, ours.

Unsinn (-[e]s), *m.,* nonsense; — **Wust,** meaningless rubbish.

unten, below.

unter, under, among.

unterbrechen (a, o), to break off, interrupt.

Unterschied (-[e]s, -e), *m.,* difference.

unterschiedlich, severally, first one then the other.

untersuchen, to investigate, examine.

unterweisen (ie, ie), to instruct, teach.

unverloren, not lost, sure.

unverständlich, unintelligible, incomprehensible.

unverwandt, unmoved, motionless.

unwillkürlich, involuntary.

Urkunde (-, -n), *f.,* record, document.

Urteil (-[e]s, -e), *n.,* lot, judgment, sentence.

V

Vater (-s, *"*), *m.,* father.

verachten, to despise, have contempt for.

Verachten (-s), *n.,* contempt, disdain.

verächtlich, contemptuous.

verändern, to change, alter.

verbleichen (i, i), to grow pale, fade; **verblichen und ergrünt,** at once faded and renewed.

verblüfft, astonished, dumfounded.

verbrechen (a, o), to break (a rule), transgress.

verdammt, accursed.

verderben (a, o), to ruin, spoil.

verdorben, *see* **verderben.**

verdienen, to deserve, merit, earn.

verdriessen (o, o), to vex, annoy.

verdriesslich, vexed, annoying.

Verdruss (-es), *m.,* vexation, annoyance; **Verdrüssen,** *special plural* (77, 30).

vereinigen, to unite, join.

verehren, to honor, revere.

vereinen, to unite, assemble.

verfassen, to compose.

verfluchen, to curse.

verführen, to lead astray, seduce.

vergeben (a, e), to forgive.

vergebens, in vain.

vergehen (verging, vergangen), to pass away, fade away.

vergelten (a, o), to requite, give retribution.

vergessen (a, e), to forget; **vergessene** (*tone*), deserted.

vergesslich, forgetful.

vergeuden, to squander, lavish.

Vergunst, *f.*, permission.

verheissen (ie, ei), to promise.

verhüten, to prevent, hinder.

verirrt, confused.

Verkauf (-[e]s, "e), *m.*, sale.

verkehrt, wrong, reversed.

verkennen (verkannte, verkannt), to mistake (one), be mistaken; **verkannt,** done wrong, mistaken.

verklagt, accused.

verklärt, radiant.

verlachen, to ridicule, mock.

verlangen, to desire, demand.

Verlangen (-s, –), *n.*, desire.

Verlanger (-s, –), *m.*, supplicant, wisher.

verlassen (ie, a), to leave, forsake; **sich –,** rely.

Verlauf (-[e]s), course, progress.

verleihen (ie, ie), to award, confer.

verletzen, to transgress, violate.

verlieren (o, o), to lose.

vermacht, bequeathed.

vermählt, wedded, married.

vermehren, to increase.

vermeiden (ie, ie), to shun, avoid.

vernehmen (a, vernommen), to hear, perceive, learn; **vernommen,** examined.

verneigen, to bow, courtesy.

Vernunft, *f.*, reason, fairness.

verrennen (verrannte, verrannt), to cross; **verrannt,** went wrong.

verrichten, to do, execute.

Vers (-es, -e), *m.*, verse, stanza.

Versammlung (–, -en), *f.*, assembly.

verschämt, ashamed, modestly.

verscheiden (ie, ie), to depart, expire.

verschieden, different, several.

verschlafen (ie, a), to sleep over, sleep off.

verschliessen (o, o), to shut up, lock up.

verschlossen, *fig.*, narrow-minded, unresponsive, sodden.

verschnaufen, to breathe, recover breath.

verschwinden (a, u), to vanish.

versehen sein, to be assured.

versessen, crazy about (something).

versetzen, to change, transfer; **in der Singschul' . . . versetzt,** you'll talk quite differently (81,11).

versichert, assured.

versingen (a, u), to sing wrongly; **versungen,** outsung.

versohlen, to sole shoes.

verspotten, to mock.

Verstand (-[e]s), *m.*, understanding, reason.

verstecken, to cover, hide.

verstehen (verstand, verstund, verstanden), to understand.

verstellt, displaced.

verstohlen, secretly.

verstossen, driven out of.

verstund, *see* **verstehen.**

versuchen, to essay, attempt, try, tempt.

vertauschen, to make over into, change.

vertan, outdone.

vertieft, absorbed, sunken.

vertragen (u, a), to bear.

Vertrauen (-s), *n.*, trust, confidence.

vertraut, familiar, well known.

Verwandlung (-, -en), *f.*, change of scene, transformation.

verwechseln, to mix up, change, alter, confuse.

verwehren, to defend, reject.

verweilen, to remain, linger.

verwirrt, confused, dazed.

verwischt, vanished.

verwundert, surprised.

verzehren, to consume.

verzeihen (ie, ie), to pardon, excuse.

verzögern, to delay.

verzwacken, to break (the rhythm).

verzweifelt, desperate, despairing.

viel, much, many, very.

vielleicht, perhaps.

Vogel (-s, "), *m.*, bird.

Vogelgesang (-[e]s, "e), *m.*, song of birds.

Vokal (-[e]s, -e), *m.*, vowel.

Volk (-[e]s, "er), *n.*, people.

voll, full, whole, complete, filled.

vollkommen, complete, perfect.

Vollmond (-[e]s, -e), *m.*, full moon.

von, from, of, by.

vor, before, in front of.

vorbei*kommen (kam, o), to go by, pass.

Vordergrund (-[e]s), *m.*, foreground.

vor*geben (a, e), to permit, allow (32, 11).

vor*haben (hatte, gehabt), to intend, have on hand.

Vorhang (-[e]s, "e), *m.*, curtain.

vorig, former.

Vorläufer (-s, -), *m.*, forerunner, precursor.

vorlaut, officiously.

vorn, in front.

vornehm, aristocratic, proud, superior.

vor*schlagen (u, a), to propose, introduce.

vor*sehen (a, e), to look out.

Vorsicht, *f.*, caution, foresight.

vorsichtig, cautious, prudent.

Vortrag (-[e]s, "e), *m.*, performance, rendering, execution.

vor*tun (tat, a), to excel.

vorüber, over, past.

vor*ziehen (zog, gezogen), to go forth; *fig.*, prosper.

W

wach, awake, waking.

wachen, to watch, wake.

Wachs (-es, -e), *m.*, wax.

wachsen (u, a), to grow, wax.

Wächter (-s, -), *m.*, watcher.

wackelig, rickety.

wackeln, to shake, fly.

wacker, stout, valiant, worthy.

Waffen-Ritt (-[e]s, -e), *m.*, war parade.

wagen, to dare, venture, strive for; **gewagt,** venturesome.

Wahl (-, -en), *f.*, choice, election.

wählen, to choose, elect.

Wahn (-[e]s), *m.*, madness, illusion, state of mind, spell, trap.

wahnbetört, fancy stirred.

wahr, true, regular.

wahrlich, truly, indeed.

wahr*nehmen (a, genommen), to perceive, behold.

während, during, while.

wahrhaftig, truly, in truth, really.

Wahrtraum-Deuterei, *f.*, dream-interpretation.

wahr*weisen (ie, ie), to direct aright.

Waisen, *m. and f.*, rhymeless lines (*see* Introduction).

Wald (-[e]s, ‟er), *m.*, forest, woods.

Waldespracht, *f.*, forest splendor.

walken, to beat soundly, pound (one another).

wallen, to undulate, course through the veins.

walten, to rule, dispose of.

Wand (-, ‟e), *f.*, wall, partition.

wandelbar, fickle.

wandeln, to wander, go.

wann, when.

Wappen (-s, -), *n.*, weapons, coat of arms, escutcheon.

ward, *see* **werden.**

wären, *see* **sein.**

warm, warm.

warten, to wait.

warum, why.

was, what, which, that which, why.

Weber (-s, -), *m.*, weaver.

wecken, to arouse, wake.

weder, neither; - ... **noch,** neither ... nor.

Weg (-[e]s, -e), *m.*, way, road.

weg, away.

Weh (-[e]s, -e), *n.*, woe.

wehren, to hinder, check, prevent.

Weib (-[e]s, -er), *n.*, wife, woman.

Weibchen (-s, -), *n.*, little wife, mate.

weich, soft, yielding, gentle, pliant.

weichen (i, i), to yield, retreat.

weihen, to consecrate, dedicate.

weil, because, since, while.

Weile, *f.*, while, space of time.

weilen, to delay, stay.

Wein (-[e]s, -e), *m.*, wine.

weise, wise, learned.

Weise (-, -n), *f.*, manner, mode; *tech.*, melody, scale.

weisen (ie, ie), to show, teach, point.

weiss, *see* **wissen.**

Weisung (-, -en), *f.*, directions, instructions.

weit, far, wide.

weither, from afar.

welch, what, which, some.

welsch, Italian, foreign.

Welle (-, -n), *f.*, wave, billow.

Welt (-, -en), *f.*, world.

weltlich, worldly, secular, profane.

wen, whom, he *or* him whom.

wenden (wandte, gewandt), to turn, change matters.

wenig, little, few.

wenigstens, at least.

wenn, if, when, as soon as, in case, provided that.

wer, who, whoever, he who.

Werbelied (-[e]s, -er), *n.*, suitor's song, trial song.

werben (a, o), to woo, sue, try (for), contest.

Werber (-s, -), *m.*, wooer, suitor, candidate.

Werbgesang (-[e]s, ‟e), *m.*, trial song.

Werbung (-, -en), *f.*, wooing.

werden (wurde *or* a, o), to become, become of; *fut. aux.*, will.

werfen (a, o), to throw, cast.

Werk (-[e]s, -e), *n.*, work, production.

Wert (-[e]s, -e), *m.*, worth.

wert, worthy.

Wesen (-s, -), *n.*, being, nature, character, mind.

Wette (-, -n), *f.*, wager, competition.

wetten, to wager, bet.

Wettgericht (-[e]s, -e), *n.*, tribunal, judges.

Wettgesang (-[e]s, "e), *m.*, trial song.

wichsen, to wax.

wichtig, weighty, important.

wie, how, as, than, like, as if.

wider, against, contrary to.

wieder, again, anew, otherwise.

wiederholt, repeatedly.

wieder*kehren, to return.

wieder*kommen (kam, o), to come again, return.

wies, *see* **weisen.**

Wiese (-, -n), *f.*, field, meadow.

wild, wild, reckless.

Wildnis (-, -e), *f.*, wilderness.

will, *see* **wollen.**

Wille [Willen] (-ns), *m.*, will, mind, design.

willig, voluntarily, willing, ready.

willkommen, welcome.

winkend, inviting, beckoning.

Winternacht (-, "e), *f.*, winter night.

Winterzeit, *f.*, winter time.

wir, we.

wirbt, *see* **werben.**

Wirken (-s), *n.*, works, achievements.

Wirre[n], *pl.*, confusion, perplexity.

wirren (o, o), to twist, perplex.

wischen, to wipe.

wissen (wusste, gewusst), to learn, ascertain, know.

Witwer (-s, -), *m.*, widower.

Witz (-es, -e), *m.*, joke, jest.

wo, where, when, if.

woher, whence, where.

wohl, well, perhaps, indeed, probably, I presume, I wonder, I suppose.

wohlbekannt, well-known.

wohlgereimt, well written, well composed.

wohlgesäumt, richly sewn.

wohnen, to dwell.

Wolke (-, -n), *f.*, cloud.

wollen (wollte, gewollt), to wish, have the intention, will, claim.

wonach, whereafter, after which, that for which.

Wonne (-, -n), *f.*, delight, rapture.

Wonne-Gewühle (-s, -), *n.*, heart's rapture, pent up passion.

wonnig, rapturously, gloriously.

wonniglich, delightful.

Wort (-[e]s, "er *or* -e), *n.*, word.

wovor, before which, from what, whereat, of what.

Wucht, *f.*, weight, bulk.

wühlen, to root, rend.

Wunder (-s, -), *n.*, miracle, wonder; **das nähm' uns doch –,** that were surprising.

wunderbar, wondrous, wonderful.

Wunderbaum (-[e]s, "e), *m.*, enchanted tree.

Wundernacht (-, "e), *f.*, magic night.

wundern, sich, to wonder, think strange, be surprised.

wunderschön, wondrously beautiful.

Wunsch (-[e]s, "e), *m.*, wish, desire, whim.

wünschen, to wish, desire.

Würde (-, -n), *f.*, dignity, honor.

würdig, worthy.

würgen, to choke, throttle.

Wurst (-, "e), *f.*, sausage.

Würzkrämer (-s, -), *m.*, grocer.

Wust (-[e]s), *m.*, trash, rubbish;
Unsinn -, meaningless rubbish.

wütend, angrily, raging.

Wutesbrand (-[e]s, "e), *m.*, fire
of wrath.

Z

zagen, to tremble, fear.

Zahl (-, -en), *f.*, beat, count.

zählen, to count.

Zank (-[e]s), *m.*, quarrel.

zanken, to quarrel.

zart, tender, gently.

Zarte (*tone*), tender, gentle.

zärtlich, tender.

Zauberspruch (-[e]s, "e), *m.*, magic
spell.

Zehe (-, -n), *f.*, toe.

zehn, ten.

Zeichen (-s, -), mark, token.

zeigen, to show.

Zeile (-, -n), *f.*, line (of writing).

Zeit (-, -en), *f.*, time, times.

Zeitvertreib (-[e]s), *m.*, pastime,
diversion, joy.

Zelt (-[e]s, -e), *n.*, tent.

zerfallen (zerfiel, a), to fall to
pieces.

zergehen (zerging, zergangen), to
vanish.

zerhackt, whacked.

zerprügelt, thoroughly beaten.

zerreissen (i, i), to tear.

zerrissen, torn.

zerrinnen (a, o), to flow; **wie gewonnen, so zerronnen,** lightly
come, lightly go.

zerschlagen (u, a), to break to
pieces, break.

zerstreuen, to disperse, scatter,
disturb.

Zerstreutheit, *f.*, absence of mind,
distraction.

Zeter (-s), *n.*, murder, death.

Zeuge (-n, -n), *m.*, witness.

zeugen, to bear witness, testify.

Zeugnis (-ses, -se), *n.*, witness, evi-
dence.

ziehen (zog, gezogen), to draw,
pull, attack, attract, go.

Ziel (-[e]s, -e), *n.*, goal, purpose,
desire.

ziemlich, quite, tolerably.

ziere, graceful, pretty.

Zierat (-[e]s, -e), *m.*, grace notes,
embellishment.

Zimmt (-[e]s), *m.*, cinnamon.

Zimmtröhren (*mode*), cinnamon
stick.

Zinngiesser (-s, -), *m.*, pewterer.

zieren, to decorate, ornament, adorn.

zierlich, splendid, graceful.

zittern, to tremble, shake.

zog, *see* **ziehen.**

Zögernis, *f.*, (the act of) tarrying,
delaying.

Zopf (-[e]s, "e), *m.*, back hair, queue,
pig-tail.

Zorn (-[e]s), *m.*, anger, wrath.

zu, to, into, along with; at, in,
too.

zucken, to start, quiver.

Zuckerkand (-[e]s), *m.*, rock
candy.

zuerst, first.

zu*geben (a, e), to yield, grant (in an argument).

zu*gehen (ging, gegangen), to take place, go on, occur.

zugleich, at the same time, together.

zu*hören, to listen, pay attention.

zu*kommen (kam, o), to come to, belong to.

zu*lachen, to laugh away.

zuletzt, at last, at the end.

zum = zu dem.

zumal, especially.

zu*merken, to go ahead and mark.

zunächst, next, first.

zu*nehmen (a, genommen), to increase, improve, prosper.

Zunft (-, "e), *f.*, guild.

Zunftberatung (-, -en), *f.*, trial session.

Zunftgericht (-[e]s, -e) *n.*, guild tribunal.

zupfen, to nudge.

zur = zu der.

zurück, back.

zurück*bleiben (ie, ie), to remain behind, fall short of.

zurück*kehren, to turn back, return, come back.

zurück*kommen (kam, o), to come back, return.

zusammen*ziehen (zog, gezogen), to draw together.

Zuschauer (-s, -), *m.*, spectator.

zu*schliessen (o, o), to close, lock up.

zu*sehen (a, e), to look at.

zu*singen (a, u), to sing on; proceed (in singing).

zu*sprechen (a, o), to award, judge.

zu*springen (a, u), to spring forward, go at it (a fight).

Zustimmung (-, -en), admiration, approval.

zu*stopfen, to put an end to.

zuviel, too much.

zuvor, first of all.

zuvörderst, first.

zu*wenden (wandte, gewandt), to turn toward; incline to.

zwacken, to pinch, cheat.

Zwang (-[e]s), *m.*, force, compulsion, constraint.

zwar, indeed, to be sure, namely.

zwei, two.

zweieinig, agreed, in peace.

Zweig (-[e]s, -e), *m.*, branch, bough.

zweite, second.

zwiefach, twofold.

zwingen (a, u), to force, compel, obtain, gain.

zwinkend, twinkling.

zwischen, between.

Zwischenspiel (-[e]s, -e), *n.*, interlude.

Zwist (-[e]s, -e), *m.*, discord, quarrel.